ANTON CHE

Three Sisters

A study-guide by

Michael Pennington

NICK HERN BOOKS
London
www.nickhernbooks.co.uk

A Nick Hern Book

Chekhov's Three Sisters – Page to Stage
first published in Great Britain in 2007
as a paperback original by Nick Hern Books Limited,
14 Larden Road, London W3 7ST

Chekhov's Three Sisters
copyright © 2007 by Michael Pennington

Page to Stage series
copyright © 2007 by Nick Hern Books Limited

Michael Pennington has asserted his right
to be identified as the author of this work

Cover design: www.energydesignstudio.com

Typeset by Country Setting, Kingsdown, Kent CT14 8ES
Printed and bound in Great Britain by Bookmarque,
Croydon, Surrey

A CIP catalogue record for this book is available
from the British Library

ISBN 978 1 85459 899 8

The edition of *Three Sisters* quoted throughout
is the translation by Stephen Mulrine published
in the Drama Classics series by Nick Hern Books:
copyright © 1994 by Stephen Mulrine

The Page to Stage Series

Written by established theatre professionals, the volumes in the *Page to Stage* series offer highly accessible guides to the world's best-known plays – from an essentially theatrical perspective.

Unlike fiction and poetry, the natural habitat of the play is not the printed page but the living stage. It is therefore often difficult, when reading a play on the page, to grasp how much the staging can release and enhance its true meaning.

The purpose of this new series, *Page to Stage*, is to bring this theatrical perspective into the picture – and apply it to some of the best-known, most performed and most studied plays in our literature. Moreover, the authors of these guides are not only well-known theatre practitioners but also established writers, giving them an unrivalled insight and authority.

Contents

From Page to Stage

This volume on Chekhov's *Three Sisters* is part of a series with the overall title *Page to Stage*. It is a good title, but we should perhaps consider what it implies. When I was a student of English Literature in the 1960s (before the days of widespread university drama courses) there was quite a sharp division between those who thought a play was for reading, like a novel, and those who like myself believed it was primarily for performing. I had a tutor at Cambridge with whom I studied Arthur Miller's *Death of a Salesman* as part of the Tragedy Paper. Every week we discussed the play's themes and structure and imagery, and to some extent its social background. One day my tutor came to see a production of the play in which I was by chance appearing at the time. I looked forward to our next tutorial. At its start he commented that Mrs Loman, in making a bed, had neglected to tuck in the blanket on the side nearest the audience: this, he felt, proved the laughable inadequacy of theatre practice in the face of a great play. And now, he said, opening the text with evident relief, let us continue with our study of it.

Times have changed a great deal. The ever-increasing enthusiasm shown by teachers and academics for live performance as the final measure of a play is quite disconcerting to those of us who have never doubted it. Theses are written on theatrical trends; books are dedicated to recording the history of performances and productions. Often actors and directors rather than literary critics are invited to lecture on the subject of drama to students; and I suppose that very few teachers would now recommend reading a play without simultaneously imagining it on the stage.

Most new plays – and all plays were once new – are performed before they are read by the public, and then published in the light of their first performances, which have usually necessitated some revisions of the original. Shakespeare was never particularly interested in the publication of his work, and what has come down to us is often an assembly drawn from prompt copies or from the memories of the actors he worked with: in other words, a strange amalgam of versions, which vary according to whether the play was being performed in the open-air Globe Theatre, in an indoor theatre, in Court, or on tour. Nevertheless, as we all know, these composite texts are endlessly studied and analysed, more or less as if they were definitive.

It may be that with the works of Anton Chekhov there is, in this regard, a particular problem. He is one of the least 'literary' of great dramatists, and for many years was not studied in the classroom or much subject to textual criticism. Now that he is, it is right and possible to discuss the milieu in which he wrote, the imagery he used, his themes, and so on. Thus you can establish that *Three Sisters*, written as the nineteenth century gave way to the twentieth, uncannily anticipates the upheavals that would engulf Russia within a generation. Obviously enough, Chekhov is showing how a social class and their way of life is gradually going under, so that the Natashas and even Kulygins of the future may become more powerful than the Prozorovs of the present. He does this in an unusually spare and lucid vocabulary. But the essential things about Chekhov are less tangible. He wrote about life as it is lived, and was specially interested in human behaviour, paradoxical and unpredictable from moment to moment. He is the most questioning and ambiguous of great dramatists: it is as if he was unable to propose one thing without also implying its opposite. He had an extraordinary ability to extend understanding to his least sympathetic characters and to criticise the most obviously attractive, thus creating a fine balance of sympathy in his audience. Though they have great emotional outbursts, these people only rarely say precisely and conclusively what they mean. This is not necessarily because they are deceitful, but because of their human inability to know fully what it is. It depends, as in life, on what is happening at the time.

So his plays are particularly elusive when read, while being extraordinarily powerful when performed well. The occasional critical essays one can find on *Three Sisters* tend to take a judgmental, two-dimensional view of the characters, as if they were essentially one unchanging thing, not several. So Kulygin the schoolteacher is described as a pompous bore, Lieutenant Colonel Vershinin as a romantic, Irina Prozorov as a sentimental young girl; but the fact is that Kulygin is also sociable and courageous, Vershinin is unscrupulous and Irina can be realistic and highly self-critical. I have heard Andrei's momentary hymn to his children's future at the end of his great speech in Act Four described as ridiculously naive. No doubt, from an objective point of view, it is: but in the theatre it is moving for that reason. We recognise the determination with which Andrei briefly rises above his suffering and expresses faith against all odds.

These figures from the distant Russian past are, in other words, much the same as we are, and as difficult to assess as the people close to us. They are sometimes one thing, sometimes another, sometimes both at once; they sometimes behave incomprehensibly even when we think we know them well; and they are always what life has made them into, not what they would ideally wish to be. The best way to experience them, I would say, is with an open mind, allowing them to remind us of our own acquaintances and our own experience of life, rather than by worrying about what they 'represent'. To see a character on a stage poised uncertainly between one course of action and another – whether to pursue a woman, or whether or not to hang up his coat – tells you far more than I can write or you can get from reading the moment on the page. It is perhaps no accident that in Chekhov's own day, once this play was established and popular, Muscovites used to speak not so much of going to see a performance of *Three Sisters* but of going to visit the Prozorov family.

So my method in writing this book is to recount the narrative from the characters' own point of view as they speak and react to each other. I have kept to a reasonable minimum the moments when I break off to say what the staging, designing and acting alternatives are, since I hope they are implied by the thoughts and feelings I describe. As far as these practical decisions are concerned, in a sense they come with the territory: though the process whereby a piece of text becomes a living thing is a complex business overall, its essentials are quite simple. If there are twelve people on the stage, the director has to place them in such a way that we can see them all, especially if they are going to speak a good deal. The set designer has to provide a realistic space for this to happen, whether working on a large proscenium stage, a small one, one which thrusts into the auditorium with audience on three sides, or in a still more informal set-up. Much of the time, common sense dictates.

From the actor's point of view, it is a byword in our profession that you must play your character from his or her own point of view – it is for the audience, not us, to make moral judgements if they want to, and the best we can do is not to exaggerate or comment. Additionally, the moment that a director casts one actor in a part rather than another, he is buying into his or her underlying personality, which will always be slightly different from another's: both actors may make very good Vershinins, but in slightly different ways, just as two painters' treatment of the same landscape will be different.

And finally, Chekhov was very clear in his instructions within the script, both on interpretative and practical matters. He frequently complained that characters cried too much in productions of his plays: he has indicated when he wants them to and how, sometimes drawing a distinction between crying and speaking 'through tears', and twice insisting in this play that Irina weeps 'quietly'. Masha, he says, wears black; Irina wears white. A designer could of course put them both in red, but it might be better to assume that Chekhov knew what he was doing.

For the central fact of the theatre is that once actors pick up the page and take it to the stage, start moving about, speak the lines to each other rather than silently to themselves, react to each other's tone of voice and interpret the look in their eyes, surprising things happen. This is where a play begins its journey; and its outcome will be as unpredictable as any journey in life.

Anton Chekhov

A BRIEF LIFE

Anton Pavlovich Chekhov was born in Taganrog, on the Sea of Azov in Southern Russia, on 17 January 1860. This was the date by the Russian (Julian) calendar, which was twelve days behind the Western calendar in the nineteenth century and thirteen behind in the twentieth (the Russian calendar is used throughout this book). His father's father was a peasant who had, exceptionally, managed to save enough money to buy his family their freedom from serfdom, so that they were able to begin to move up into the merchant class. Chekhov's father was a grocer; he was also very religious and tyrannical, and Chekhov later said that because of the paternal beatings and constant religious observances, there had been no childhood in his childhood.

The future writer was the third of six children (a seventh died in infancy). His two elder brothers, a talented writer and artist, became respectively alcoholic and consumptive, and their father was bankrupted when Anton was fifteen. The family escaped to Moscow, except for Anton, who stayed at home to complete his schooling and look after their affairs before coming to Moscow to study medicine at the University. Then he supported them by writing humorous articles and short stories for the city's magazines, learning the comic observation and economy so characteristic of his later work.

Throughout his life Chekhov practised as a doctor. His work in the communities where he lived – first of all near Moscow and later in Yalta in Southern Russia, where he moved after being diagnosed with tuberculosis in 1897 – was exceptional. He assisted in alleviating famine, cared for local peasants, helped forestall a cholera epidemic, conducted a district census, and opened three schools and a post office. In 1890 he travelled with great difficulty across Siberia to the prison colony on Sakhalin Island, off Russia's east coast, to make a thorough survey of conditions there, personally interviewing each of its ten thousand convicts. The publication of his subsequent report, *The Island of Sakhalin*, slightly influenced government policy.

Though he was attractive to women throughout his life, we know for certain of only one major relationship, with Olga Knipper, the leading actress of the Moscow Art Theatre, whom he met at rehearsals for *The Seagull*. Their lives were marked by long separations – the sick Chekhov in Yalta, Olga working on his plays in Moscow – and is well known to us because of their moving correspondence, most of which has survived. The couple married in Moscow in 1901: there were no children.

By the time he married Chekhov was very ill. When *The Cherry Orchard* opened on his birthday in 1904, the audience and his colleagues were shocked by his frailty; in May of that year he left Russia for Germany with his wife, and died (immediately after drinking a final glass of champagne) on 2 July 1904, in Badenweiler. His body was brought back to Moscow in a refrigerated car marked 'For Fresh Oysters'; his funeral procession became confused with that of a general, and he was finally buried in the Novodevichy Cemetery in Moscow, where his grave can still be visited.

Writing 'Three Sisters'

Despite predicting that it might turn out to be 'boring Crimean rubbish', Chekhov settled down to write *Three Sisters* in the autumn of 1900, after nearly a year of believing that though he might have a theme he had no idea how to dramatise it. As he complained to Olga Knipper, the new play would look sadly up at him from his desk as he looked sadly back at it, and from time to time one of his heroines would suddenly 'go lame'.

Behind him at this point were twenty years as a writer of short stories, some of which are still regarded as masterpieces in the genre. However, though he had had success with one-act farces and monologues, several of which are still performed, his first three full-length plays had been far from successful. There was an unperformed early piece which we now know as *Platonov*; *Ivanov*, which was only a moderate success; and *The Wood Demon*, a failure which he nevertheless used as the basis for the later, greater *Uncle Vanya*. In 1896 *The Seagull*, generally thought to be his first major play, was premiered in St Petersburg with an unsuitable company and inadequate rehearsal and was more or less booed off the stage. During the following year *Uncle Vanya* succeeded in Russia's provinces, and in 1898 Chekhov, after much hesitation, authorised a revival of *The Seagull* by the newly-formed Moscow Art Theatre: it was a triumph. Soon he was being seen as Russia's leading dramatist, and his subsequent career until his death in 1904 was inseparable from this company, who then presented a revived *Uncle Vanya* and his last two plays, *Three Sisters* and *The Cherry Orchard*.

THE MOSCOW ART THEATRE

The Moscow Art Theatre (MAT) was led by the director Vladimir Nemirovich-Danchenko and the actor Konstantin Stanislavsky. At the time of its founding, Russian theatre was stuck in outdated styles of acting and melodramatic situations. The star actor or actress was seen as the most important element, there was no such thing as a director in our sense, and the author was not much regarded – the poster for the first production of *Ivanov* had carried Chekhov's name in tiny lettering compared to those of the actors and the date. Chekhov disliked this as much as his new colleagues, though he was not entirely innocent of the old faults. Both *Ivanov* and *Platonov* have traditional features, such as a huge central part complete with several monologues addressed to the audience, and a fatal gunshot at the end. The MAT gave him the chance to find his true and lasting voice. The company was insistent on certain principles that our modern theatre takes for granted – a director-led ensemble would have adequate rehearsal time, the star performer would be less important than the team, and the mood of a play should be expressed by careful design and the delicate realisation of relationships between the characters. It was perfect for Chekhov's style: the collaboration on the revived *Seagull* was a huge turning-point for all concerned. The six remaining years of Chekhov's short life (he died at forty-four) confirmed both their and his place in theatre history: until very recently the MAT curtain carried the emblem of a seagull.

Nevertheless Chekhov had many reservations about the company's style, which he often found gloomy, slow and over-reverent. He particularly disliked their elaborately created 'real' sound effects – and no doubt, pre-dating recorded sound as they do, they would strike us as pretty crude as well; but they were achieved with great ingenuity. For instance, the sound of a mouse scratching behind the wainscoting of a wall was done by actors standing in the wings and rubbing their hands on toothpicks made of goose quills. And for all his suspiciousness, Chekhov knew that he had found the right circumstances for his work at last.

WRITING FOR THE ART THEATRE

His involvement with the MAT means that, with *Three Sisters*, Chekhov is writing for the first time specifically for colleagues he knows – in fact he was shortly to marry its leading actress,

Olga Knipper. His old schoolfriend Andrei Vishnevsky was already in his mind to play Kulygin the schoolteacher. And in a particularly vivid example, Vsevolod Meyerhold, who was to play Tuzenbakh, was, as the character would be, of German parentage, and had taken Russian nationality a few years before (in the event Meyerhold left the cast before the opening). So, like Shakespeare and Molère before him, Chekhov was to some extent able to tailor his characters to the particular talents of his actors. In a playful letter, he promised Vishnevsky that he would be able to wear a frock coat and a ribbon with a medal on it around his neck, while he warned Olga Knipper that she would have to pay him ten roubles for writing her such a good part, or he would give it to another actress.

During the arduous period of composition, certain influences on his thinking are evident. As a young man he had spent a long summer holiday in a garrison town where one of his brothers had a job as a teacher. He noticed how the army officers liked to break up their dull routine with long sessions of philosophical debate. It was not what was said but the energy of the argument that kept them going. In *Three Sisters* Chekhov extended this idea by suggesting that such philoso- phising could also be used as the means of seduction by which Vershinin precipitates the tragedy of Masha Prozorov. In his book *Understanding Chekhov*, Donald Rayfield has also pointed out that Chekhov had been reading about the Brontë family, with their three sisters and failed brother, children of a power- ful father and forgotten mother; and also to the fact that Chekhov had himself been involved with no fewer than five families of three sisters in his life.

LOCATION OF THE PLAY

The other significant difference between *Three Sisters* and his earlier plays is that Chekhov breaks with his own habit as to its location. It is still quite a shock to remember the limited range of people and places about which he generally wrote. *The Seagull*, *Ivanov* and *Uncle Vanya* are set in a part of Russia that, though not spelt out, is fairly easily identified as the central provinces towards the south of the country, between

Moscow and the Crimea, on old estates now struggling to remain viable. With *Three Sisters*, Chekhov had another idea: it is, uniquely, set 'in a large provincial town'. He does not name it, but immediately on completing the play he wrote to his friend Maxim Gorky that he was imagining a place like Perm, which is on the edge of the Ural mountains that separate European Russian from Asia, seven hundred miles northeast of Moscow. At that time there was no direct railway link to Moscow, only a twice-weekly connection with St Petersburg (two days' travel), and precious little with anywhere else in the region. The area is far less easy of access than southern Russia, and less temperate: Olga Prozorov complains of the late arrival of spring right at the start of the play.

The sisters' town is sizeable enough – Andrei Prozorov speaks of a hundred thousand inhabitants. But in other ways the characters might as well be in Siberia; and from the outset the practical difficulty of getting to Moscow is made clear. This is counterpointed all the time with the undeniable fact that as well-off young people they could achieve it if they really tried. This paradox becomes central to the play: they could change their lives but they don't. The tubercular Chekhov was living in the south of Russia, about the same distance from Moscow as was Perm; he missed Moscow life (and Olga Knipper) a great deal, and is writing a play about exactly that longing.

A SETBACK

On 23 October 1900, Chekhov undertook the long journey to Moscow with his new script to read it with the assembled company. They seem to have found the play difficult, even saying it was impossible to act, or that it was not so much a play as 'a prospectus'; one actor said he disagreed with the author 'in principle'. Stanislavsky reports that Chekhov was particularly perturbed because he thought that he had written a comedy, whereas everyone took the play as a 'drama' and wept at it, so that he thought he had quite failed in his intentions. This matter of definition was a chronic problem between him and the company. He had a general habit of sub-titling his plays, however serious, as comedies, as he did *The Seagull* and

The Cherry Orchard, or at most as 'Scenes from Country Life' (*Uncle Vanya*): *Three Sisters* is the only one (somewhat belying his complaint) described as 'a drama'. It is also true that while he insisted to the MAT that it was 'light-hearted, a comedy', he was describing it to other people as 'gloomier than gloom'.

REHEARSALS

In any case, by 11 December Chekhov had had enough of these misunderstandings and was on his way to Nice, where he rewrote sections of Act Three and, particularly, Act Four. From here he corresponded anxiously with the actors and director about the progress of rehearsals, which had now begun. He is pleased to hear from Olga Knipper that she has found the right walk for Masha. On the other hand, he is annoyed to hear that the play's Olga keeps taking Irina by the arm and walking her about: 'Can't she get around on her own?' Perhaps more importantly, he had left behind a personal friend, an army Colonel, to ensure there was no 'slackness' among the actors in matters of military uniform, bearing or officer behaviour – there had already been a rumour that the play was critical of the army, and Chekhov was eager to dispel suspicion. Unfortunately the plan misfired a little: the Colonel objected to the fact that Vershinin had an affair with a married woman in the play, which he said could not happen. Chekhov's view of the army was generally favourable: he believed it was on a cultural mission, going into outlandish parts of Russia with 'knowledge, art, happiness and joy', and he was afraid that the officers might be played in a clichéd way – 'the usual heel-clickers with jingling spurs'. He wanted them presented as simple, decent people, dressed in worn, untheatrical uniforms, without military mannerisms.

IN PERFORMANCE

Chekhov was still abroad, in Rome, when the play opened on 31 January 1901. The press reviews were mixed, but the public rapidly took it to their hearts, and in fact it was to be the first of Chekhov's plays to make him substantial sums of money.

He didn't see the production during this first season; but when it was revived in September 1901 he took a far more active part than he had ever done before in rehearsals. By this time he was married to Olga Knipper, whose colleagues teased her that the play should be re-titled *Two Sisters*, Chekhov having stolen the third. Some of his interventions are documented. He worked continuously with the actor Vasily Luzhsky to improve his performance as Andrei, going over every line in detail with him: he insisted for instance that in Andrei's major speech in Act Four he should become so excited that he is almost ready to punch the audience. He demanded that the portrait of the Prozorovs' father which hung on the wall of the set should be changed as it looked too Japanese. He also insisted that the Act Three firebell should have a particular small-town sound, not that of a Moscow firebell – it should be a 'soul-searing provincial fire alarm'. It's a very good point, difficult but not impossible to realise in a modern production. The bell is heard moments after Irina has poignantly cried 'Moscow . . . Moscow' at the end of Act Two, so this is a typically Chekhovian counterpoint, underlined a moment later when Ferapont harks back to the 1812 fire in Moscow. Dissatisfied in general with this third act, Chekhov re-staged it. Some of the actors complained that he was not much help, being inclined to answer their more intellectual queries by saying simply that Andrei should wear slippers, or that someone else should whistle. But to me he sounds like a very perceptive modern director, and he was rewarded by much better reviews in the press.

Themes

Chekhov once observed that the real drama of a person's life goes on inside them and has little to do with external events, which are generally random. And in reality the sufferings of the three Prozorov sisters and their brother, which they blame on their distance from their beloved Moscow, are to do with their own characters and half-understood feelings. Their real tragedy is in the relationships they form. Masha falls in love with Vershinin, but he moves on, as he was surely always going to, and leaves her stuck with her unloved husband. Irina accepts the kindly Tuzenbakh, and she becomes a widow before she is a bride. Andrei fails to see the consequences of marrying Natasha, whose only real attraction is that she offers him an escape from everything his family expects of him. All of them gain some self-knowledge in the end (which gives the play its tragic depth). Andrei eventually manages to voice his desperation, and therefore begin to cope with it, while Olga, repressed for much of the play, becomes strong enough in the moving final moments to sustain and comfort her sisters.

So the central characters' unease is not purely geographical, though they certainly feel displaced. The military are genuinely en route, waiting for their next posting, while even after eleven years of living here the Prozorovs are convincing themselves it is only temporary. Apart from the elderly servants, only two characters, Natasha and Kulygin, are truly local, fully adapted, and consequently have the strength to pursue their destinies single-mindedly – she to look ruthlessly after her own interests and, as she sees it, those of her children, and he obstinately determined to put up with his wife's love affair for the sake of a face-saving future. To an extent, Chekhov's plays are all built on such lines – what happens to the residents (usually the smaller characters) when the visitors arrive for a time and then leave.

Much as they hanker after the past, the Prozorovs are also, to some extent, victims of a somewhat un-Russian emotional reticence. Some things simply aren't spoken about enough in this family. At the very start Olga mentions their father's death, but Irina cuts her off:

> Why bring it all back?

Later, Masha opens up about her passion for Vershinin, but Olga can only keep blocking her:

> That's enough. I'm not listening to you anyway . . . I don't care. I can't hear you. You can say whatever stupid things you like, I'm not listening.

The ensuing scandal in Masha's life – her affair with him – is never spoken of onstage by the other sisters; even at the terrible moment of Vershinin's and Masha's parting, Olga can only keep urging:

> Stop it, stop . . . Masha, that's enough, please don't, darling.

Not dwelling on their miseries seems to be a point of honour – if only they did, rather than complaining they are not in Moscow all the time. Perhaps the father has not been mourned in quite the right way. General Prozorov is hardly mentioned after the reference to the anniversary of his death at the start: he is alluded to once by Vershinin, and then somewhat negatively by Andrei. So he is buried in more senses than one. As for the mother, she is barely referred to either – she is little more than the owner of the ornament Chebutykin smashes (and possibly his long-dead lover), and even Masha says she is already forgetting what she looked like. Losing a parent can liberate even the most loving children, but this has not happened here – they have done little since he died, least of all the son Andrei. One of the daughters continues her unwelcome career teaching children, another (potentially the most gifted) works in the telegraph office and then for the council; the third, a talented musician, struggles on in a wretched marriage, escaping only for a heartbreakingly brief affair. There is nothing much for them to be proud of: it is as if they had been stopped in their tracks, cut adrift from the healthy cycles of life and death.

For those outside the family there is still less hope. Doctor Chebutykin has cut himself off from life: at one point alcohol mercilessly forces him to see the consequences of this, but he returns in the end to a cruel indifference towards everyone except Irina. Kulygin, Masha's husband, manages to hold on to her, but has little to look forward to, and there is no particular sign that he understands that it is partly his doing that Masha has fallen for Vershinin. Vershinin may well act in the same way at his next posting; Tuzenbakh dies. These last two, in their evident interest in the future of Russia, construct a broader philosophical frame for the play as they dream of a time when everyone will understand the purpose of their lives. But this is mocked by their own destinies: Tuzenbakh's love for Irina leads to his destruction in a pointless duel, while Vershinin and his family go on apparently unaffected to Poland.

Clearly enough, the four Prozorovs are the ones we are likely to care about most in reading or watching the play. But Chekhov ensures that our sympathy sometimes flows away from them. There is no doubt that their chronic nostalgia involves some snobbishness. Most notably, when the outsider Natasha arrives as Andrei's guest at the lunch party in Act One, her choice of dress is criticised to her face by Olga. This unkind remark from a well-bred and educated hostess provokes her victim's long-term revenge, as we are made to remember towards the end when Natasha in turn criticises Irina's clothes sense. Olga helps with the fire in Act Three, but at the same time her inability to deal with intimate matters is shown: as Natasha attacks the old servant Anfisa, the feebleness of Olga's protests is disappointing. Always their longing for Moscow is lyrically expressed – the repeated cry of 'Moscow . . . Moscow!' is what everyone remembers about this play – but it is well and truly discredited by Vershinin, who, with a well-chosen anecdote about an imprisoned government minister, proves that once they are actually in Moscow they won't find it so special. However, though he may well be right, it is difficult to like him for this: Chekhov is making the critical point while ensuring that we keep our affection for the sisters and our respect for what they think they want.

The play was written at the turn of the century, just ahead of great upheavals in Russia, and it is laced with a subtle form of political comment. If the Prozorovs represent a privileged past, Natasha (though intensely bourgeoise and far too maternal to be a socialist) looks forward to a new world – a more soviet one in that her thinking is more efficient and less sentimental, but one much reduced in spirit. These opposed attitudes to life rehearse big Russian issues in a domestic setting. More explicitly, Tuzenbakh speaks prophetically about the great storm that will shortly blow Russian life clean of boredom and laziness, and Vershinin responds (when he wants the attention) with talk about a glorious future when good-hearted people will form the majority. He sees less clearly than Tuzenbakh: the more we get to know the Prozorovs, the greater our intuition that they will soon be as out of place here in the Urals as they would be in Moscow or as émigrés in Western Europe.

Himself about to marry, Chekhov is also interested in the problems of unhappy marriage: Andrei and Natasha, Kulygin and Masha, are clearly ill-matched. By contrast, Chekhov hints, Irina's and Tuzenbakh's fateful but kindly union – or indeed Olga's modest certainty that she would even marry an old man as long as he was good – might make a better basis for marriage than the deluded romanticism that is ruining the others' lives. Chekhov is also concerned with what happens to a family when the male figurehead loses authority. Within a year of his father's death, Andrei is beginning to falter, despite his sisters' hero-worship. But as he gradually falls under Natasha's control, the sisters' failures become all too obvious as well. Colonised by their ruthless sister-in-law, they gradually abandon their own interests, and in the end, their dreams. At the start they speak of Moscow as 'our home, you see', even saying they will be returning in the autumn, but by the end of Act Two Olga and Masha have stopped talking about it, and even Irina is no longer naming a date.

Chekhov's Technique

Chekhov conveys all his insights in this play with, even by his standards, a new technical mastery. From the very opening, he uses a subtle counterpoint: as Olga longs to return to Moscow, a fragment of conversation is heard behind her like a coincidental comment:

CHEBUTYKIN: Oh, forget it!
TUZENBAKH: It's nonsense, of course.

As Irina and Olga then repeat the same dream, the men happen to laugh; and when Olga says how much she would have loved her husband if she had found one, Tuzenbakh is heard saying to Soliony:

Honestly, you talk such nonsense, I'm fed up listening to you.

And in fact this technique works both ways. Just as strong emotion can be undercut by overheard fragments of talk, the tone can suddenly change from fun to naked emotion: the little scuffle about Chebutykin's inappropriate present of a samovar to Irina is suddenly silenced by a pathetic outburst from him. This method ensures that nobody's feelings, however sincere, can definitely be taken at face value: there is always another point of view, and we are kept at a slight distance. Irina, lying in bed in the morning, dreams of a life of useful work; Olga does such work but it doesn't make her happy. Tuzenbakh laughs at Vershinin for philosophising but soon does it himself. Before we see him, Andrei is built up as the star of the family, but when he arrives all he really does is complain. Everything is relative. In the next act, Andrei exclaims to Ferapont that he longs to be in Testov's or the Great Moscow Restaurant, even though he knows the old man is as deaf as the Siberian wind.

The whole play is dotted with moments of terseness that seem bald on the page, but are truly powerful when acted. Chekhov, supported by his new company, is more than ever sensing the theatrical force of a single word or phrase in the right place. So Masha's dawning interest in Vershinin is expressed simply by the removal of her hat and one lifelike remark, funny and revealing:

I'll stay for lunch.

Then Tuzenbakh, in full idealistic flight, has his high-flown ideas punctured by Chebutykin:

Baron, you've just said that people will look up to us, but we're pretty small all the same. (*Stands up.*) Look how small I am, for instance.

But in the next act, Tuzenbakh himself does something similar to Vershinin, ending their grand discussion about life with the laconic:

Meaning? . . . Look, it's snowing – what does that mean?

Sometimes a simple remark made at the beginning of the play remains in our memories long enough to be echoed at its end. At the start Olga says:

Yes, I'd have loved my husband.

– and in Act Four Andrei, who has exchanged the loneliness of bachelorhood for the painful solitude of his marriage, comments on the same subject with the same simplicity:

My wife's my wife.

This, by the way, is not to do with translation: the Russian can be even more monosyllabic. Chebutykin's dismally repetitive catchphrase 'It's all the same' is just as terse in Russian (*vsye ravno*). And he responds to Masha's anxious questions about whether the Baron might survive the duel with Soliony by evading the question:

CHEBUTYKIN: Joking aside, this'll be his third duel.
MASHA: Whose?
CHEBUTYKIN: Soliony's.
MASHA: And what about the Baron? (*Chto u barona.*)

Chekhov is also becoming a master of what, in musical terms, is known as 'diminuendo'. After the fire in Act Three, life gradually returns to its normal rhythms, but keeps being interrupted by bursts of individual need. When Masha confesses that she loves Vershinin, part of its unwelcome quality is that a new pulse of feeling is starting just as everyone is at last ready to go to bed: then, when that is settled, the self-justifying Andrei inappropriately arrives, blustering and breaking down. The drunken Chebutykin bangs on the floor. As that crisis relapses, time can once more be heard ticking on, undisturbed. Finally Irina confirms that the army will soon be leaving and calmly decides to marry Tuzenbakh. It is as if she alone is thinking at the right speed, on a steady rhythm: it is only in such quietness that such a big decision can be made. The result is a new maturity, economy and emotional depth which makes *Three Sisters* perhaps the most popular of this great quartet of plays.

SUBTEXT

Subtext is a word heard almost daily in modern rehearsals. Essentially it means the unwritten thoughts or emotional truth beneath what a character says. These may be quite different from what is being verbalised; and since in life we often don't say exactly what we mean, audiences are quick to understand the phenomenon on the stage – as long as the actor implies the subtext strongly by tone of voice or physical attitude.

In Chekhov's drama, perhaps for the first time, subtext is crucial to our understanding of what is going on. In Shakespeare, for example, there is little subtext. When Hamlet says:

To be or not to be; that is the question

– he is perfectly expressing the thought that is in his mind. As a general rule in fact, Shakespearian characters do say what they mean – indeed he lends them his own articulacy to make it unequivocal. The exceptions come when a character is simply lying, and we know he is. And of course in Shakespeare there is always the device of the soliloquy to the audience when even a dishonest character is absolutely truthful about what they feel.

But when, in Act One of Chekhov's *Seagull*, Trigorin is made to feel awkward by excessive praise, he says:

> There must be a lot of fish in that lake.

It is a fairly obvious example, and therefore funny: he is clearly covering his embarrassment with small talk. In the last act of *The Cherry Orchard*, there is a more poignant example. Lopahin and Varya meet by arrangement: we know that he wants to propose to her, and that she wants him to, but he loses courage and they talk about the weather, so the opportunity is missed. In the first act of *Three Sisters*, Masha puts on her hat and is about to leave the party when Vershinin arrives. She greets him with no particular friendliness. A few minutes later, having listened to him talk, she takes off her hat and says she'll stay for lunch. This is charming because the subtext is clearly that she likes him and wants to spend more time in his company.

The love affair that she and Vershinin then embark on gives rise to a very pure form of subtext in the utterances of Masha's husband Kulygin, as he struggles to make the best of his situation. In a state of permanent anxiety about his wife's loyalty, he constantly says how good she is and how much they love each other, even when it is entirely inappropriate to be talking about her at all. He is always superficially jolly, but even the Latin tags with which he peppers his talk become more and more ominous. A study of some of his speeches during Act Four provides wonderful examples: he will not say what is on his mind, but his instinctive choice of subject and imagery leave us in no doubt of his unhappiness.

CHEKHOV'S LEGACY

Three-and-a-half years after the opening of *Three Sisters* Chekhov was dead, at forty-four, of the tuberculosis which had plagued him, and which he had kept as secret as he could. In the interim came *The Cherry Orchard*, which anticipates political change in Russia still more acutely, plus a few stories – but that is all. From a humble beginning as a provincial shopkeeper's son and lacking the social advantages of many of his contemporaries – Tolstoy, Turgenev – he had become a leading figure, though it is probably true that at his death he was still more acknowledged as a fiction writer than as a dramatist, a situation which is now reversed. His theatre work was, almost from the start, original enough to be disliked and misunderstood, as the Petersburg premiere of *The Seagull* demonstrates, and he always depended on the vision and loyalty of his colleagues and audiences to win over his critics.

A century later, what baffled those critics has become a standard by which much present-day drama is measured. We are still taken aback at how completely Chekhov suspends moral judgment and allows his characters to speak for themselves. The seeming inconsequentiality of some of the dialogue, and the comedy which is never far from the surface of the most intensely dramatic situations, remains startling and refreshing; associating him with such great later playwrights as Samuel Beckett and Harold Pinter. He has a perception about political life which informs his plays without turning them into propaganda or making them less human. He has a deep feeling for the gap between human ambitions and any ability to realise them, and an acute sense of human foible. Chekhov believed that a play should reflect the inconsistencies of life, and that we often conceal our most urgent emotions behind the commonplace activities of eating, drinking and chattering. His genius is to allow these ordinary rhythms to seem to proceed in their own way, while subtly organising them so that everything contributes to the play's forward movement. Nothing is wasted in *Three Sisters*. Beneath the apparent non sequiturs, understatements and evasions lies the profound poetry of life.

His influence has been pervasive but subtle, and the adjective 'Chekhovian' is applied to writers who seem very little like him or each other, such as David Mamet, Tennessee Williams and Alan Ayckbourn. The same adjective is sometimes used to describe revivals of certain plays of Shakespeare – a unique retrospective compliment. Such is the fascination of his characters that whole plays have been written about their imagined lives outside the text, such as Helen Cooper's *Mrs Vershinin*, and Brian Friel's *Afterplay*, which proposes a meeting in later life between Andrei from *Three Sisters* and Sonya from *Uncle*

Vanya. Actors and directors seek opportunities to perform Chekhov as avidly as they do Shakespeare. The fact that his work has been played in so many different spaces and styles – naturalistic, expressionist, politically explicit, lyrically sentimental – only proves its strength. And all this is based on four dramas set in a narrow range of Russian society in the last few years of the Tsarist dynasty. Working within these limits, Chekhov's insight, subtlety, passion and wit nevertheless changed future audiences' expectation of the theatre.

Act One

In a large Russian provincial town, it is shortly before lunch on 5 May, the name-day of Irina Prozorov, the youngest of the three daughters of the late General Prozorov. A name-day in Russia is not necessarily the same as a birthday, but is celebrated as vigorously: Irina is named after Saint Irene. As it happens, what should be a happy occasion is also the first anniversary of General Prozorov's death.

All three sisters are in the drawing room, beyond which can be seen the large ballroom traditional in such houses, where the table is being laid for lunch, and into which three of their guests will shortly wander. From the women's conversation, led by Olga Prozorov, we gather a number of contradictory details. When the General died last year there was snow on the ground (and then sleet while he was buried, which perhaps accounted for the poor turn-out of mourners); but this year the day is bright and sunny. On the other hand the birch trees are still not out, which reminds Olga that at such a time in Moscow, where they were brought up, everything would be in blossom by now.

All the sisters have complicated reactions to these memories; what unites them is a desire to go 'home'. It will emerge that their mother died even before their father, and that Olga, the eldest, is still only twenty-eight. They are now having to manage on their own in a situation which in any case was never easy for them: the move here eleven years ago was the unavoidable result of their father's appointment as commander of a brigade, but it sharply cut them off from their emotional roots in Moscow. Their desire to sell up and return now is sharpened by Olga's gloom at having spent the last four years working as a teacher in a local girls' high school, a life she finds unendurably exhausting – she has already 'started to think like an old woman'. Even today, on her sister's name-day, she is in her uniform, correcting her pupils' exercise books as she walks and talks.

Irina sees no reason why the family shouldn't return. Their brother Andrei will be a Professor soon, it seems, so will surely welcome the move for his work: only Masha, the middle sister, is stuck in this place, for reasons we do not yet know, but she could at least come and visit them in the summer holidays. Masha's situation remains a mystery for the time being because she says not a word during this opening conversation, but sits in black, reading and whistling to herself – a tasteless thing to do, in Olga's view.

High spirits have transformed Irina: Olga comments that she looks specially beautiful. Masha looks beautiful too, she says; and their brother Andrei 'could be quite handsome', but has put on weight recently. Olga's emotions are moving this way and that as she speaks: what she describes makes her happy enough, but she also feels acutely that she has lost her own bloom through overwork. On balance, 'everything is fine'; but then again, perhaps it would have been better if instead of working she'd 'got married and stayed home all day':

> *A pause.*
> OLGA: Yes, I'd have loved my husband.

The sisters' lunch visitors are officers from the brigade stationed nearby. Lieutenant Tuzenbakh, who is a Baron, Staff Captain Soliony, and an army doctor, Chebutykin, now drift into the main, upstage room. Tuzenbakh, apart from wanting to escape from Soliony's conversation, has forgotten to tell the sisters that they will be receiving their first visit today from his commander, Lieutenant Colonel Vershinin. Olga's and Irina's reactions are nicely contrasted, one polite and the other romantically direct:

> OLGA: Really? That'll be nice.
> IRINA: Is he old?

At 'about forty, forty-five at most' (quite old in this company) Vershinin is obviously viewed by his colleagues with respectful amusement. Tinkering on the piano (Chekhov's diversionary ploy to make the giving of necessary information seem natural, not stagey), Tuzenbakh gives the girls a light-hearted warning.

Vershinin is on his second marriage, he has a mother-in-law
(as most married men do, but Tuzenbakh's mention of the fact
makes her seem slightly ominous), and as well as demonstrating a philosophical turn of mind, he may bore them with
tales of his two little daughters and his wife. She is an affected
woman by all accounts, who wears a pigtail and frequently
attempts suicide, apparently to keep her husband on his toes.
This is probably hearsay – oddly enough Tuzenbakh seems
not to have encountered Vershinin socially, though he will
presumably have done so in the line of duty: he uses the
phrase 'by all accounts' to preface the fact that Vershinin is 'a
decent chap'. The one thing against him is that, rather like his
wife, he 'talks too much' – which, as we shall see, is rich
coming from Tuzenbakh. Tuzenbakh himself would have left
such a wife, he claims; however we shall see in the play that
one of his main qualities is constancy in love.

Soliony, meanwhile, is announcing an odd and immaterial fact
to Chebutykin:

> Now, with one hand I can lift fifty pounds – but with two,
> a hundred and eighty, possibly two hundred. And from that
> I conclude that two men aren't just twice as strong as one,
> but three times, or even more.

Chebutykin retaliates, equally irrelevantly, with a recipe for
baldness he has found in the newspaper. He determines to
make a note of it:

> . . . nine grammes of naphthalene, in a half-bottle of
> alcohol . . . to be dissolved, and applied daily . . . better jot
> that down.

He even seems about to outdo Soliony by going on to some
chemical formula that involves corks, glass tubes and alum,
but we never learn what it is. He is interrupted by Irina, still
in her most buoyant mood:

> Ivan Romanych, dearest Ivan Romanych!

As these two greet each other, the atmosphere becomes suddenly animated: there is obviously the strongest attachment

between the doctor, nearly sixty, and the twenty-year-old girl. Irina seems quite liberated by his presence:

> It's as if I'm sailing, with a wide deep sky above me, and great white birds flying past. Why is that? Tell me, why?

Chebutykin fondly echoes her words:

> (*Kisses both her hands, tenderly.*) My little white bird . . .

In fact this is the morning, Irina claims, that she suddenly has the answer to how to live – it is:

> as if everything in life had suddenly become clear to me . . .

Her answer is intensive work. The very idea of it (and perhaps only the idea) brings her joy, and she describes it in the play's longest sustained speech so far:

> A man must labour, he should work in the sweat of his brow, no matter who he is, and that's the only thing that gives meaning and purpose to his life, the source of all his happiness and joy.

These admirable sentiments lead her into a little hyperbole:

> Oh, it must be wonderful to be a workman, to get up when it's still barely light, to break stones on the road . . .

We might wonder how Olga, so fatigued with actual labour, might be reacting to this. But before Irina goes too far she hints at a little self-knowledge:

> Dear God, better to be a dumb ox, or a horse, if only to work – anything but a girl who gets up at twelve o'clock, takes her coffee in bed, and then spends two hours dressing!

Chebutykin goes along with this: he will, as she demands, 'refuse to be my friend' if she fails to start work soon, and Chekhov specifies the tone in which he warns her of it:

> (*Tenderly.*) That's exactly what I'll do.

Olga, however, is tougher, gently puncturing Irina's rapture by confirming that Irina herself is, near enough, the oversleeping

girl she describes. Though brought up by their military father
to rise at seven, Irina has now rather fallen apart:

> Nowadays Irina wakes at seven, and then lies thinking until
> at least nine o'clock. And with such a serious face! (*Laughs.*)

The laugh may be a little unfair. A good choice for the actress
of Irina at this point is to imply that she was aware of that
when she said it herself – if she is surprised by Olga's remark,
it makes her less self-critical than she really is and even rather
silly. Nevertheless, we can see that she is still very young when
she goes on to protest:

> You think it's strange if I look serious. But I'm twenty!

Like Chebutykin, the audience should feel for her enthusiasm
(hoping it lasts) and respect her seriousness.

Tuzenbakh now speaks at length, as Irina did: for all his
comments about Vershinin, he is clearly not averse to philosophical talk himself. Well-born, he believes that idleness in
Russia will soon be dispelled by the 'fierce, cleansing wind'
that he senses 'blowing up', and all her citizens will be hard at
work, 'every one of us'. From the way his speech is con-
structed, we understand the personal reasons for this prediction: he has some inkling of why it might come true. In fact
he is in rebellion against his privileged upbringing in St
Petersburg, which excluded him from joining any workforce: as
a child his boots were pulled off by manservants; he was
indulged by his mother; there was no tradition of work in his
family or need for it. Rather than being grateful for this shel-
tering from life's realities, as no doubt many of his friends
were, he admirably rejects it, and is now, in theory at least, a
socialist before his time. Tuzenbakh is one of the few characters in Chekhov instinctively able to look into the future and
glimpse such cataclysmic Russian events as the 1905 and 1917
revolutions that led to the founding of the Soviet state:

> . . . I shall work, yes, and in twenty-five or thirty years'
> time, everyone will work. Every one of us!

It is hardly his fault that his optimism seems naive to us; not
his fault either that unless they manage to emigrate, the work

much of his 'reactionary' class will end up doing will be breaking stones in a labour camp. And in fact Alexander Solzhenitsyn, the great Russian writer and critic of the Soviet regime, would start his period of forced exile in the kind of brickworks Tuzenbakh hopes will save his soul.

Chebutykin's function at the next moment is simple: he debunks both Irina and Tuzenbakh with a speech as terse as theirs were long-winded:

> Well, I shan't work.

Tuzenbakh, like a good tennis player, changes direction and swiftly gives him tit for tat:

> You don't count.

Even less sympathetic than Chebutykin, the eccentric Soliony now joins in, ignoring the main subject altogether:

> In twenty-five years' time you won't even be alive, thank
> God. In another couple of years you'll die of a stroke.
> Either that or I'll lose my temper and plant a bullet in your
> brain, my angel.

Soliony seems to be aiming this mock-threat at Chebutykin, but it could equally be at Tuzenbakh: as the story develops this would make some sense. Whichever is decided on in production, it is a little unnerving and out of place, especially since Soliony then unexpectedly sprinkles scent from a little bottle onto his chest and hands.

Thus the interesting debate started by Tuzenbakh and Irina is thoroughly disposed of: we have rapidly moved from the virtues of work towards some hint of meaningless violence. Though peaceful himself, Chebutykin is making a slightly negative impression as well, though he does have age and a certain charm on his side. He now claims not to have opened a book since leaving university, preferring the newspapers, from which he habitually notes down his little scraps of useless knowledge. It is as if he was collecting enough just to get by socially, his knowledge forever superficial and his real convictions unreadable.

There is a knocking from the room below, perhaps the servants' quarters, and Chebutykin, seeming to know it is a signal for him, abruptly departs, 'stroking his beard'. The awful thought that he might be about to present some elaborate name-day gift to Irina occurs to Tuzenbakh, but it is immediately interrupted by Masha's first utterance. She murmurs the opening of a poem by Alexander Pushkin, *Ruslan and Lyudmila*, well-known to educated Russians as the story of a young man's efforts to rescue his kidnapped bride:

> 'By a curving shore stands a green oak tree, Hung with a golden chain . . . Hung with a golden chain . . . '

With this, she puts on her hat and prepares to leave, an odd thing to do during her sister's name-day celebration. Clearly she is, in her way, as unpredictable as Soliony. Promising to come back in the evening, she sounds a note of nostalgia similar to that of Irina and Olga earlier: today, when they can only muster two or three visitors for a name-day party, compares badly with the time when their father was alive, and:

> we'd have as many as thirty or forty officers arriving, and the noise . . .

Perhaps it is the inescapable pain of this memory that is driving her from the house, though she is obviously making matters worse by the very act of leaving. She 'laughs tearfully', and Olga finds herself 'in tears' at the memory, though Irina clearly thinks she should overcome the feeling and support her as the youngest sister:

> Well, really . . .

However the 'horrible, frightful' Soliony is always on hand as a distraction from such emotions, and he interrupts this little awkwardness between the sisters. First he offers a nonsensical hint about the difference between men's and women's conversations, and then, as if not to be out-quoted by Masha, drops in a line from a fable by Ivan Krylov (the Russian equivalent perhaps of Aesop), *The Peasant and the Workman*:

> 'Before he had time to gasp, the bear had him in its grasp.'

The air seems suddenly full of obscurities, and this perhaps is how Soliony likes it – his preference seems to be to unsettle everyone. Masha, irritated, takes it out on Olga:

Stop howling!

The arrival of the name-day gift of a cake from Protopopov, a man 'from the council', thus breaks a tricky deadlock. It also introduces us briefly to a new element. We are meeting the elderly Ferapont, described by Chekhov as a 'watchman from the council' and, as it turns out, quite deaf; and Anfisa, the family's eighty-year-old nanny. In terms both of Russian life-expectancy at the time, and of the age-range of the play's other characters, this is quite something: the sisters are all under thirty, and Anfisa is as much as a generation older than their dead parents.

The gift she now ushers Ferapont in with seems not particularly welcome. This Protopopov is clearly disliked, especially by Masha, who affects not to remember his name properly: it is unusual and disrespectful in Russian not to refer to someone by their first and second (patronymic) name as well as their surname, but he will remain simply 'Protopopov' throughout the play. However there is worse to come – Chebutykin's surprise gift, as self-conscious a gesture as they all feared: he is presenting Irina with a samovar on her name-day, which is a little like giving her a large electric toaster. It seems to be in such bad taste, in fact, that Olga immediately flees from the room. It is difficult to understand how it could be shocking enough for that: perhaps she has a rather exaggerated sense of propriety. Tuzenbakh, Irina and Masha are more amused than anything else:

IRINA: Dearest Ivan Romanych, what are you doing?
TUZENBAKH (*laughs*): I told you!
MASHA: Ivan Romanych, you've absoutely no shame!

However Chebutykin is quite overcome by the embarrassing failure of his expression of love for Irina, and we can see that it doesn't take much to make him feel worthless:

My darling girls, my sweet girls, you're all I have . . . I'll be sixty soon, I'm an old man, a lonely, useless old man.

There's nothing good about me, except the love I have for
you . . .

This outburst, the most emotionally candid of the play so
far, is surprising, pathetic, even shocking; and we see that
Chebutykin's habitual flippancy veils much deeper feelings.
He may also, of course, be working them up a little for effect.
Irina has the kindness to insist that the only problem with the
samovar is that it is too generous as a gift:

But why give me such expensive presents?

This is well-judged by her – she is more of a diplomat than
either of her sisters – because it allows Chebutykin to recover
and save face by pooh-poohing her:

(*Through tears, angrily.*) Expensive presents! . . . (*Mimicking
Irina.*) Expensive presents . . .

*

At this point what could be thought of as the play's prologue
ends. It has laid the ground for the action proper: we have the
impression that Vershinin, about to arrive, will be a man who
makes things happen. It has taken between ten and fifteen
minutes of stage time to introduce the audience to all but four
of the principal characters. Like any dramatist getting his play
going, Chekhov has had a good deal to achieve. He has needed
to get across to the audience what they have to know, but never
in such a way that his technique is obvious and certainly not at
the expense of natural lifelike behaviour in his characters –
Tuzenbakh softly played the piano as he introduced the
subject of Vershinin. More subtly, he has done it by mixing
actual facts with apparent incidentals. The opening line of the
play could hardly have been more blunt: the date, the anniversary of the death. But the effect was immediately softened
by seemingly random information – there is no real need for
this to be Irina's name-day, but it is interesting that it is, and it
allows everyone to have their different reactions to it. It is
obviously a sad anniversary, but this is conveyed largely by the
memories the sisters share as if they were snapshots – the snow

falling, Irina's faint, the clock striking, the sleet – in contrast with her cheefulness now and the good weather.

The director has to allow matters to develop at an unhurried pace: there is much for the audience to acclimatise itself to, and this is a world far more distant from us than it was from the play's original audience. There are also quite a number of contrasting characters to get acquainted with. As far as the men are concerned, it is already clear that Soliony is the oddity in the group, and difficult for us to understand as yet: his manner of address ('my angel') is sometimes strange, and his tone both menacing and ridiculous. But since none of it seems to bother his colleagues, we follow their example and let it go. The other eccentric seems to be Chebutykin. The opening exchange between him and Soliony may seem silly and trivial, but it reveals important details of character. Soliony is boastful and likes to disconcert; Chebutykin often avoids what is being said to him by turning his attention to his little notebook or his newspaper.

As for the actresses, they have a double job to do. Important information has to be conveyed clearly. But there are strong and quite unstable emotions involved as well – nostalgia, sadness, the day's high spirits – and the three sisters are easily affected by each other. In fact they all feel several things at once. Masha is dressed gloomily but seems contented enough in her silence. Irina awoke in high spirits because it was her special day but this reminded her of when she was small in Moscow and her mother was still alive – so her happiness is touched with a sense of loss. And of course all three must be thinking of their father. Meanwhile Olga's reminiscence reveals something of her character in contrast to Irina's. It is almost an issue between them: Olga tends to look back but Irina tries not to. Bluntly she said:

Why bring it all back?

And in all of them, there is a counterpoint between significant speech and casual action: Masha sat reading and whistling, and Olga corrected schoolbooks as she talked. Life seemed to be moving along at its own unpredictable rhythm, though it was all carefully organised by Chekhov.

Once joined by the men, Irina soon introduced one of the play's main subjects of discussion – the importance of work, a belief wholeheartedly expressed by several characters who don't do much of it. Chekhov deals in obvious 'themes' only very subtly – he is always more interested in human behaviour – but this is certainly one of them. And in terms of Irina's and Tuzenbakh's characters, there is more than one thing to be felt by the audience: the actors should create amusement at their innocence but respect for their ideals. Throughout the play, in fact, the production needs to be alert for anything in the text or stage directions that contradicts the obvious, any subtle points that reveal more than they appear to.

*

Vershinin is announced by Anfisa with a slight sense of complaint – lunch is being delayed by his arrival – but resoundingly by Tuzenbakh. Briskly announcing himself, the newcomer is immediately the cause of great excitement, especially since he seems to know a good deal about the two sisters standing before him. Bluntly he exclaims:

> My, how you've grown . . . But surely there should be three sisters . . . I certainly recall your father, Colonel Prozorov, having three little girls . . .

To Irina's delight, Vershinin is not only from Moscow, but once served in General Prozorov's brigade. For some reason Masha's welcome is more subdued, even distant; when Vershinin thinks he recalls her from the old days, she says frankly:

> Well, I don't remember you!

As if to retrieve the excited atmosphere, Irina hurries to bring Olga in, and this jogs Vershinin's memory – he is sure now of their names and sequence in age, though not much more. As for their father:

> I need only close my eyes, and I can see him, as large as life.

Having been so young, the girls would hardly remember Vershinin; but Masha has the longest memory, even if she seems the least friendly. Olga and Irina are reciting the comforting name like a mantra:

> IRINA: From Moscow? You're from Moscow? . . . Olya!
> Olya! . . . Lieutenant Colonel Vershinin is from Moscow,
> would you believe . . .
> OLGA: You're from Moscow? . . .
> IRINA: Aleksandr Ignatyevich, and you're from Moscow . . .
> that really is amazing! . . .

– and they blurt out what sounds less a dream than a definite plan:

> OLGA: We'll be moving there, you see.
> IRINA: Yes, we should be there by autumn, we think.

Introducing some reality, Masha suddenly does recall something. It may be embarrassing for Vershinin, though he takes it in good grace: he was much teased in the old days for being 'the love-sick major' (though he was only a lieutenant). Masha goes on to regret the ravages of time:

> Oh, and you've got so much older!

Altogether, Vershinin might be quite taken aback by his welcome: Moscow may not mean so much to him. He may also not realise that he is being fallen upon because he is the only one of the family's visitors to invite some comparison with the past: it is as if their father was still alive in him. Gradually, however, his reception begins to inspire him. Noting in passing that he once lived on the same street as the family – Old Basmanny Street – he plucks a melancholy string, as Masha did. He remembers a gloomy bridge over the Moscow River, where you could get:

> quite depressed, if you were on your own

– but it is really so that he can make a cheering contrast:

> Still, the river here's so wide, so majestic! A superb river!

He obviously has a knack for touching on something sad, perhaps to arouse sympathy, and then moving swiftly off it.

Whether or not the sisters are affected by this, they want to play down his praise for their environment, since for them everything in Moscow is better than anything here. Olga counters with:

Yes, but it's cold. It's cold here, and the mosquitoes ...

Vershinin's reproach is quite blunt:

Nonsense! It's fine and healthy, a good Russian climate.

Clearly he is going to have little patience with the sisters' nostalgia: he loves everything here, especially 'the gentle, modest birch'. Perhaps sensing a resistance to his appreciation, he moves on: the only incongruous thing in the perfect picture is the fact that the railway station is fifteen miles away from the town.

Perhaps Soliony has been longing for a chance to interrupt. He makes a remarkably silly joke:

Well, I know why.
Everyone turns to look at him.
It's because if the station were nearer, then it wouldn't be so far, but since it's far, that means it isn't near.

Chekhov asks for '*An awkward silence*'; the question is, how awkward? Not for the last time, the company has to decide whether they take Soliony in their stride, knowing his odd ways, or if he is really embarrassing. Tuzenbakh, ever helpful, breaks the silence by calling him 'a great joker'. But one virtue of his interruption is that it has given Olga time to think. Now that she is getting accustomed to Vershinin, her memory clicks into place:

Now I've remembered you too. I do remember.

Vershinin confirms her memory. He knew the girls' 'dear mother', now buried in Moscow's great Novo-Devichy Cemetery, remembers her well, whereupon Masha laments that she can't say as much:

Would you believe, I'm already beginning to forget her face. We won't be remembered either. We'll be forgotten.

This melancholy thought is a philosophical cue for Vershinin, if Olga did but know it: it gives him a chance to muse on the passage of time. Off he goes. The fate of man is to proceed steadily towards oblivion, and future generations may take a poor view of what seems important now. Conversely, in the future things disregarded at present may become highly significant, just as the findings of Copernicus, who asserted that the earth moved round the sun, or Christopher Columbus, who discovered America, were originally despised. This is not quite true – although both these giant figures may have been regarded with suspicion, their work was not thought of as 'pointless and stupid', as Vershinin claims. In fact his whole argument is rather contradictory, more eloquent than meaningful. He concludes that life at present will:

> come to be seen as bizarre and uncomfortable, mindless, and none too clean, maybe even sinful.

This is enough to get Tuzenbakh going; for all his jokes about Vershinin, he too has been waiting for someone to bring out the philosopher in him. He chooses to believe that the present age may come to be be admired for progressive thought. Despite all the suffering he sees, there are compensations:

> We don't have torture nowadays, or executions, or invasions . . .

All this inconclusive talk holds little interest for Chebutykin and Soliony, and the good-natured Tuzenbakh is already struggling. Soliony seizes the opportunity to turn his eccentric sights on him:

> Cheep! Cheep! Cheep!

For the moment Tuzenbakh manages to ignore this and keep up his lofty tone:

> . . . the suffering we see around us today – and there's so much of it – even so, it indicates a certain rise in moral standards . . .

It is not a very impressive point – perhaps Soliony has thrown him off balance – and Vershinin seems to be losing interest:

Yes, of course.

In a way, having displayed his feathers, Vershinin is signing off, and it gives Chebutykin the chance to make a joke in his turn. It is all very well to say that future generations will look up to us, he says, but people will always be small – in their souls, and in his case literally:

(*Stands up.*) Look how small I am, for instance.

Tuzenbakh is stumped as effectively as he was when he spoke of the virtues of work; balanced between a joke and sadness, the conversation stalls. The momentary silence is broken by an unexpected sound, a violin playing in the next room. The philosophers' attention is caught. This is, as Masha says, Andrei, the girls' brother, the absent head and hero of the family.

Between now and Andrei's entrance we remember what we have been told about him. As Irina said, he is likely to become a Professor, which is a good reason for the family to move back to Moscow. Also he has grown stout, just as Olga has grown thin, since their father's death. But he has been curiously absent – we could have forgotten there was a brother at all. Now he gets even more of a build-up than Vershinin did. Irina declares that he is the 'brains of the family' and that he has ignored his father's military inclinations to become an academic. Masha, also championing him, hastens to correct any impression that this was the source of trouble within the family – no, it was 'Papa's wish'.

By his sisters' account, Andrei looks even better next to his new girlfriend. His interest in this local 'young lady' is partly a matter of amused sisterly puzzlement, but there is an element of social snobbishness as well. Masha goes further:

Ugh! The way she dresses! Not just unattractive and unfashionable – it's absolutely pitiful . . . No, Andrei isn't in love, I won't hear of it – he's got more taste . . .

As far as she is concerned, this unnamed girl, with her scrubbed cheeks, yellow skirt and red blouse, would find her level better by marrying the chairman of the local council, the man who sent the cake, whom again she dismissively refers to only by his surname, Protopopov.

It is Masha too who insists that Andrei join them, and calls him in. In the audience we think we know what to expect, and in a way he is the play's first surprise, perhaps even a disappointment. A reticent figure to say the least, he mops the sweat from his brow as he approaches. Proudly introduced by his sisters, he reacts to the news of Vershinin's Moscow origins with noticeably less enthusiasm, even a little sarcastically:

> Really? Well, I congratulate you, my dear sisters won't give you any peace now.

Then, as anyone might, he becomes seriously embarrassed by their continued gushing. Irina boasts that he has made a little picture frame for her special day, and Vershinin doesn't quite know what to say – maybe it is an unimpressive object:

> Yes, it's . . . it's very . . .

Not only that, but there's another frame 'over the piano', so this is a sort of production line. To his credit, Andrei dismisses it all, but the sisters are undeterred:

> He's our intellectual as well, and he plays the violin – he makes all sorts of little things out of wood. Really, he's a jack of all trades . . .

– says Olga, without adding that he might be master of none.

Feeling less and less comfortable, Andrei tries to escape: but as he may have guessed, worse is to come. The inevitable teasing about his love-life even animates the sedentary Chebutykin. The dialogue is accompanied by some humorous physical harassment:

> OLGA: He's in love! Andryusha's in love!
> IRINA (*clapping her hands*): Bravo! Bravo! Andryusha's in love!
> *Chebutykin approaches Andrei from behind and seizes him with both arms around his waist.*

CHEBUTYKIN: 'For love alone did Nature bring us forth upon this earth!'

It is all much at odds with Andrei's mood – he has slept badly, he feels restless and out of condition, and something is on his mind: as the early northern dawn came up he 'kept thinking, about this and that'. He mops his brow again and tries to change the subject. He tells Vershinin that he plans to translate a book from English during the summer, but his attitude to being able to do such a remarkable thing is surprisingly ambiguous:

. . . our father, God bless him, burdened us with an education.

'God bless him' could be sincere, or just a sardonic acknowledgment. What is Andrei's attitude to inheriting the mantle of his father? It is now fairly clear that Prozorov approved of Andrei's becoming a scholar rather than a soldier, but Andrei is not so sure about it. He feels that putting on weight since the father's death has been a matter of his body welcoming the loss of paternal discipline – at the same time he admits the idea is 'ludicrous'. To our ears, this is just a way of admitting that he has let himself go, physically and intellectually. He and his sisters speak three languages – Irina has a fourth, Italian, so the General was clearly piling it on by the time his last child arrived – but Andrei feels they are over-educated for their present position in life. Masha hastens to agree, turning the argument into a complaint about 'this town': to be so educated in such a place is as superfluous as having a sixth finger. This genuinely provokes Vershinin; no doubt he can hear snobbish laziness in it:

I don't believe it! (*Laughs.*) Superfluous!

According to him, any human community has need for 'an intelligent, well-educated' element such as this family; certainly the three of them (it is significant that he doesn't say 'four' – perhaps he is only interested in the ladies) will eventually influence a town of a hundred thousand people for the good, even if they get no benefit themselves. Indeed the difference may only be felt after the end of their difficult lives.

Clearly identifying with the inhabitants rather than them, he imagines that by some magic the number of enlightened people will multiply until:

> finally people like you will be in the majority.

In rather a large leap of thought, this leads him to believe that:

> in two or three hundred years' time, life on this earth will be unimaginably beautiful, astonishing.

– and such a paradise must be prepared for by accumulating more and more knowledge in the present.

It is a completely unprovable argument, and somewhat fanciful; but its goodheartedness reproaches Masha, with a remarkable effect. Vershinin is a good judge of his audience. The promise of significance, immortality even, at such an apparently futile moment in their lives works wonders on his younger listeners, though Olga says nothing. Irina is deeply affected in her ingenuous way:

> (*With a sigh.*) We really ought to have noted all that down.

Meanwhile, with Chekhov's wonderful understatement, Masha's quickened interest in Vershinin makes her reverse all her plans in four short words (it is equally terse in the Russian):

> (*Takes off her hat.*) I'll stay to lunch.

As for Andrei, perhaps the least easily impressed, Vershinin's eloquence has given him a chance to escape: unobserved, he has slipped away.

So it is really a matter of Vershinin and his effect on the women. It would be a good acting choice for him to lose interest in Tuzenbakh as well as the less charismatic man tries to get the philosophy going again. Tuzenbakh says much the same thing as Vershinin did, in his own manner:

> We must prepare for it, we must work . . .
> VERSHININ (*rises*): Yes. Still, what a lot of flowers you have!

Tired of abstract talk, Vershinin simply loves being in this company, in this gracious house in its beautiful setting. It is much preferable to his military lodgings with their smoky stoves and tattered furniture, which he carefully plants in the conversation:

> Yes, there's been a distinct shortage of flowers like this in my life. (*Rubs his hands.*) Ah, well, never mind, eh?

Tuzenbakh tries again, defensively announcing that he is a true Russian and so entitled to feel strongly about things:

> No doubt you're thinking, well that's just a German getting emotional. But I'm Russian, my word of honour . . . My father's Orthodox . . .

This is obviously a sore point with him, though amusing to us: insecurity about how his origins are perceived will dog him through the play. Although there is a pause, Vershinin completely ignores him, no doubt making him feel still more of an outsider, and starts 'pacing about the stage'. At first he seems to be making a new and interesting philosophical point. If only the life we are living were a sort of 'rough draft', and we had a chance to learn from it before having a second try. In his own 'fair copy' Vershinin would elect to live somewhere like this, 'with flowers, flooded with light'. No doubt Tuzenbakh knows what is coming:

> I have a wife and two little girls, and on top of that, my lady wife doesn't keep well, and so forth . . .

This fulfilment of his prediction should make Tuzenbakh feel better. But are the sisters amused, remembering the warning? Or are they so carried away by Vershinin's eloquence that he alone has their sympathy? Perhaps they have different reactions from each other. At any rate, it is a piece of wry Chekhovian humour that, now he has broached the predicted topic, Vershinin gets no chance to elaborate on it, but is immediately interrupted by a new character. It must be quite annoying for him, whether he shows it or not, to be joined now by Kulygin, a local schoolmaster.

*

Our impression that things would start to develop with
Vershinin's arrival has been confirmed. His effect on the
sisters has been powerful, and dramatic in the case of Masha,
offhand at first but soon caught up by his manner, and perhaps
by his ideas. When she bluntly declared that she didn't
remember him, the moment could of course have been played
lightly; but it will have been more interesting if her apparent
lack of enthusiasm was conspicuous. Either she is always
prickly with strangers, or, more subtly, she has been taken
aback by her immediate attraction to him, and has reacted
defensively. Significantly, Masha then fearlessly introduced
the subject of love by remembering 'the love-sick major'.
Clearly Chekhov means to connect Vershinin to the idea of
romance without delay.

Irina of course has reacted to Vershinin more innocently. Olga,
as befits the eldest sister, was polite and informative to a new
arrival, though she was also the first to query his enthusiasm
for their local landscape as opposed to Moscow. Andrei has
been no more than courteous, and as head of the family has
cut an unimpressive figure – though that could be put down to
shyness. He seems to have chosen a local girlfriend, unlikely to
be his intellectual equal, as an escape from his sisters' expec-
tations. His superior officer's arrival has inspired Soliony to
further eccentricities. Chebutykin has been part-melancholy,
part-mocking, and a certain darkness within his character has
begun to emerge: within his joke about being too small for
Tuzenbakh's conception of man's greatness was a faint echo of
significant discontent with himself.

In his plays and stories, Chekhov often satirises the Russian
love of talk for talk's sake. The impression given by Vershinin
and Tuzenbakh is of intelligent men with time on their hands,
some way from 'civilisation' and with little outlet for their
intellects. Consequently, you feel that you have listened to
some fine language but not much of an argument. Perhaps
there was a little competitiveness between them; at any rate
Tuzenbakh soon lost Vershinin's attention when the latter
sensed a more interesting audience. Vershinin was an impressive speaker, but his ideas had something vague about them,
and he may have been a little conscious of his own charm. To

contrast this house with his miserable lodgings (and in fact he is a senior officer, so how bad can they be?) sounds flirtatious, a thinly disguised plea to be adopted by the family. Between all these characters, except perhaps the outsiders Chebutykin and Soliony, we sense a web of relationships beginning to form.

*

Andrei's reluctant emergence onto the stage hardly had the impact to start a new movement for the act. But the arrival of Kulygin – the local high school boys' teacher, and in that sense the male equivalent to Olga – certainly does. His reaction to Irina's name-day has been, first of all, to put on his 'uniform frock coat', in other words to announce his own position in his profession, and once here, he more or less takes over the conversation. He has a little speech ready for the occasion:

> allow me . . . to wish you, most sincerely, from the bottom of my heart, good health

– but it comes with a slightly cautionary moral note:

> and everything a young woman of your age could hope for.

Of course he has a gift for Irina, even less appropriate than Chebutykin's samovar:

> . . . this little book. It's the history of our school during the last fifty years, written by myself.

– but it shortly turns out that he has already given it to her, the previous Easter. Before she can remind him of the fact, he hastens to greet both old friends and the newcomer, Vershinin, notifying him of his own rank – 'court counsellor'. He then boasts to Irina of the thoroughness of his book in recording the names of all pupils and ex-pupils at the school; and he rounds things off with a Latin tag, which is probably beyond them all:

> *Feci quod potui, faciant meliora potentes.* [I have done what I could, let stronger people do better.]

– followed by a kiss for Masha.

Kulygin is quite a surprise, a character as eccentric perhaps as Soliony, but more talkative. As he goes on, it is hard to know whether to laugh tolerantly at his pomposity or dislike his patronising tone. Apart from the kiss, he started out by greeting Irina as his 'sister', which surely means by marriage. He is, in fact, Masha's husband, which answers the lingering question of why she stands slightly apart and isn't fully included in the plan to return to Moscow. Since Irina already has a copy of his little book, Vershinin suddenly finds it given to him instead; it is enough to make him want to leave the company he was beginning to enjoy so much:

> (*Makes ready to leave.*) Well, I'm extremely pleased to have made your acquaintance.

More importantly, Vershinin realises that he has 'intruded' on a name-day celebration. Olga is surprised at his deference and invites him to stay to lunch, and she takes him away with her, perhaps to brief him on the family set-up and protect him from more embarrassing attentions from Kulygin.

To his reduced audience Kulygin reveals more of himself, correcting the Prozorovs' domestic arrangements *en passant* without losing the thread of his argument:

> We shall amuse ourselves, each one as befits his age and condition. These carpets'll have to be taken up for the summer . . . they'll need some Persian powder, or naphtha-lene . . . Masha loves me. My wife loves me. Yes, and the curtains should be put away along with the carpets . . .

All these things seem to be equally important to him – the love of his wife, the cleanness of his in-laws' house, and their general behaviour. It is one and the same point: everything should be in its right place, and 'form', as recommended both by his school's headmaster and by the ancient Romans (an-other Latin tag about the healthy mind in the healthy body), is one of the essentials of life. Likewise, a Sunday such as this is a day of compulsory rest – especially for those who, like himself, work especially hard – as well as a celebration for his sister-in-law. There is clearly little room for experimentation in his life or in that of anyone he attaches himself to.

Having taken things over in this way Kulygin is ready to claim Masha as well:

He clasps Masha around the waist, laughing.

If this is typical of his husbandly behaviour, it helps to explain her somewhat eccentric and erratic manner, her general stance of protest. Far from being free to go to Moscow, she is tied to endless tours of duty:

KULYGIN: Masha. We have to be at the headmaster's today at four o'clock.

Torn between frustration and a decent unwillingness to defy him in front of visitors, she briefly rebels:

I'm not going.

– but immediately capitulates. It is enough to show how very tired she is of this role. And there is worse to come:

KULYGIN: and afterwards we're to spend the evening at the headmaster's house.

We, let alone Masha, are already weary of this headmaster. But Kulygin's sense of wonder that his boss can preside over such evenings despite his ill health even leads him to admire the man's candid confession:

I'm tired, Fyodor! I'm so tired.

He pauses before repeating this unremarkable sentiment only to point out that something else should be corrected:

Your clock's seven minutes fast.

Like a punctuation, Andrei's violin is heard once again, as it was when Chebutykin pointed out how small he was: this time it is allowing us to absorb the effect, both ludicrous and chilling, of Masha's husband. For someone so taken up with his wife, there seems to be more genuine warmth and relaxation in his greeting of Olga and the news that there is a pie for lunch:

.

Ah, my dear Olga, dear kind Olga! . . . I'm tired, and today I
feel so happy.

– and he rushes off towards the ballroom without a further
thought for Masha.

His departure makes space for a flurry of reactions between
Chebutykin, Tuzenbakh and Masha, the undercurrent of
them all being Kulygin. Masha sounds more angry with
Chebutykin than she would normally be: she fiercely warns
the old man against his drinking. He claims to have been sober
for two years but there is clearly an issue here, and this brief
aside between them tells us as much as any long exchange.
Both Chebutykin and Tuzenbakh, impracticably, advise Masha
to defy her husband:

> TUZENBAKH: If I were you, I wouldn't go . . . Simple as
> that.
> CHEBUTYKIN: Don't go, my dear.
> MASHA: Oh yes, don't go . . . This damnable life, I can't
> bear it . . .

Soliony meanwhile continues to target Tuzenbakh:

> Cheep! Cheep! Cheep!

As he moves towards the lunch table, the focus swings upstage
with him. There we find Kulygin toasting Vershinin in terms
that confirm his inability ever to introduce himself without
referring to his status as Masha's husband and mentioning
how good or kind she is. Then we are back to the drawing
room, where Tuzenbakh is hanging back with Irina. For our
benefit and his, Irina spells out Masha's problem:

> She got married at eighteen, when she thought he was the
> cleverest of men. Now, she doesn't. He's the kindest, but
> not the cleverest.

Irina is also preoccupied with the rudeness of Soliony, whom
she instinctively fears. Tuzenbakh, though the butt of his jokes,
is more tolerant, attributing much of his behaviour to shyness
in public, improbably claiming that Soliony can even be 'quite

witty and charming' when he is one-to-one. The play will prove Irina a better judge of character than he is.

In any case, Tuzenbakh is more concerned with opening his heart to Irina – not for the first time, we sense. But his romantic vision of 'a long, long line of days' ahead of them seems unwelcome, though she does at least use the intimate form of his name in replying:

> Nikolai, please don't speak to me about love.

His passion for her is obviously deeply entangled with a broader longing, for work, for struggle, for value:

> . . . this thirst in my soul has merged with my love for you, Irina. It's as if by design – you're beautiful, and that's why I find life so beautiful.

Irina's response to such stirring emotions is quite complex. She objects strongly to life being described as beautiful, since in her and her sisters' case it has only been oppressive, so much so that it brings her close to tears to think about it. But she does glimpse the same way out as he does, even if it strikes her as compromised by their lack of training – a fact which, despite her years, she sees mercilessly:

> We must work, work! That's why we're so depressed, and have such a gloomy outlook on life . . . it's because we know nothing of work. We've come from people who despised work . . .

So the situation between them is not hopeless. They may not be equally matched in love – most of it seems to be on Tuzenbakh's side – but the idea of honest labour is where the two of them meet, and that can only give Tuzenbakh hope.

At this moment Natasha (Natalya Ivanovna – we never hear her family name) arrives, not in the yellow skirt and red blouse Masha described, but in a pink frock with a green belt. She is extremely nervous at being late, not yet feeling at home in this extended family and unsure quite how to behave. Worse, Andrei is not there to meet her – we have just seen him travel from his study directly to the lunch-table. There is no particular sign as yet of what Masha would call 'commonness': the fact that the whole party is already at the table would be daunting even for someone more self-confident. Certainly she feels 'terribly awkward'. She checks her hair in the mirror – a sign either of the vanity she will show later in the play, or of simple anxiety. She plants a 'firm, prolonged kiss' on Irina, which may be more than Irina was expecting, and she greets Tuzenbakh; so she has been in the house often enough before for such familiarities. Indeed the fact that she doesn't need announcing by Anfisa, unlike the newcomer Vershinin, shows that she is a frequent enough visitor to have today's choice of clothes noticed. They are certainly rather colourful; but Olga's reassurance as the hostess:

Don't be silly, we're all family here.

– suddenly becomes extremely ambiguous:

You're wearing a green belt. My dear, that's all wrong!

This must be terrible for Natasha. She hopes that Olga, superstitious, may mean it's an unlucky combination of colours; but no, she really is commenting on Natasha's bad taste:

No, no, it just doesn't match . . .

Natasha is so desperate that she tries to describe the belt as not so much green as 'sort of neutral', and she approaches the lunch table in a state of mortification and dread. It has been a setback she will never forget – or forgive.

Her trial continues unabated when she arrives there. It must seem to her as if everyone is a little drunk already, though really it is a matter of high spirits. Kulygin seems to reveal a sexual archness that we haven't seen before with his hope that Irina should soon find 'a handsome young man', but he's really expressing his wish that she join the great ranks of the married that he approves. After her brief encounter with Tuzenbakh, this is a little untimely for Irina, and she says nothing; while any talk of love brings Natasha into the firing line as well. She and Andrei are determinedly teased, Chebutykin and Kulygin in particular wasting no time:

CHEBUTYKIN: And I wish you a fine young man too, Natasha.
KULYGIN: Natasha already has a young man in mind.

These amorous hints are hardly the kindest way to welcome an outsider, but fortunately the talk drifts away again. Masha's frustration and annoyance spill over from the previous scene, and she promises to hit the bottle:

Yes, why not, let's eat and drink and be damned.

This draws a characteristic rebuke from her husband, who gives her 'C-minus for conduct' even though his own behaviour towards Natasha has not been A-plus.

Soliony breaks his silence to assure Vershinin that the fruit liqueur he is drinking is made of cockroaches, so clearly he doesn't spare his superior officer in his search for discomforting jokes; in reaction, Irina significantly comes 'close to tears', so Soliony really does bother her. Olga celebrates the fact that she is free from work all day and that another large meal is being prepared for this evening, and Vershinin, sounding as if he has no family, swiftly secures an invitation to it in a way that makes it impossible to refuse him:

Am I allowed to come too?

It may be this that forces Natasha into an embarrassed remark:

They don't stand on ceremony here.

She is undoubtedly right: neither her reception at the table, Soliony's remarks or Vershinin's begging for hospitality show much etiquette. Nobody acknowledges what she says, and her slightly gauche remark hangs in the air. Unfortunately even to open her mouth is going to provoke more teasing, and Chebutykin obliges with a line from an operetta. Andrei for once protects his girlfriend, irritably shutting him up, before two final arrivals complete the cast.

*

Party scenes or meal scenes such as this are notoriously difficult to pull off in the theatre. Each scripted line has to be

precisely placed by the speaker so that it is heard by the
audience, of course; but some of these remarks are noticed by
the other characters while some are not. There has to be a
continual impression of background noise and high spirits,
not to mention the clatter of plates and general business of
eating and drinking – all very natural but highly organised if
they are not to be distracting. It is a considerable discipline.
For an actor to improvise loud laughter at a moment when
someone else's line needs to be heard is obviously undesirable;
at the same time, there needs to be a certain amount of im-
promptu conversation (known as 'rhubarb' in the trade), the
general effect of which is noticed by the audience but not its
detail. A company of actors has to work together as exactly and
generously as they might in a team sport, listening carefully to
each other; and it is the director's job to orchestrate matters
tightly, and make sure that the performance does not change
too much during the run of the play.

This is specially important in such a scene by Chekhov. We are
finding how his technique works. A seemingly random pattern
of observations, overlapping threads of conversation and
overheard remarks – some revealing, some commonplace,
some comic – is doing as much to convey the flavour of this
group as direct narrative. The lunch party is a natural exten-
sion of this technique. Now we see everyone assembled, all in
the upstage room, framed for our inspection just as they will
be shortly for a group photograph. And what a group it is, a
community we feel we have got to know quite quickly. If you
go back over the whole of the first act it becomes clear that
there was nothing that did not make its contribution to the
carefully assembled picture. Every non sequitur was con-
nected, as it turned out; every trivial detail was necessary.

*

Now two final characters appear, Second Lieutenants Fedotik
and Rodé (a man who is established straight away as always
shouting in 'a guttural accent'). They bring good cheer and
further gifts to celebrate Irina's name-day; a basket of flowers,
a camera to record the event, and a spinning top, which
Fedotik boasts makes 'an amazing sound'. With their arrival,

assuming that Anfisa is in attendance, everyone but Ferapont is before us.

Fedotik will probably demonstrate his spinning top: its strange, haunting noise has the effect of turning Masha in on herself, and she repeats the opening lines of *Ruslan and Lyudmila* – the 'curving shore', the 'green oak tree, hung with a chain of gold' – which preoccupied her at the start of the act. But now she is more upset, tearful that:

> That line's been going through my head since morning.

Her husband, the immediate source of her unhappiness, is still labouring his points at Natasha and Andrei, drawing attention to an old superstition:

> Thirteen at table, that means there's somebody in love.

(Actually, there are thirteen only if you include Anfisa.) Chebutykin, brought in like this by his crony, rubs it in by claiming that Natasha is blushing, he 'can't for the life of me think why'. This brings the house down. Natasha has managed only one remark herself, and the teasing has been unremitting. She rushes from the table in genuine upset, pursued by Andrei, determined to head her off:

> NATASHA: I'm so ashamed . . . I don't know what's the
> matter with me . . .

It's an interesting phrase: there is nothing the matter with her any more than with anyone else. Her response to her treatment is not anger or embarrassment but shame – but at what? Her dress sense? Her inferiority socially? The fact of running away from table?

> They're making a fool of me. I shouldn't have left the table,
> it's bad manners, but I can't help it . . .

This vulnerability pushes Andrei into protectiveness. She is not to worry, all is good-natured: the company is 'harmless' (not entirely true); kindhearted (Kulygin and Chebutykin?); everyone loves both of them (untrue). It is a good effort, and he manages to get her to the window, out of the sight of everyone. Natasha is 'just not used to company', at least not this kind, and this veiled appeal calls forth more solicitude from Andrei. It comes in the form of a declaration of the most romantic love, in a manner we hadn't expected of him:

> Oh, you're so young, so beautiful, so wonderful . . . I'm so happy, my heart's filled with love and joy . . .

Within moments there is a proposal of marriage:

> My dearest, good, pure Natasha, be my wife!

Nothing is entirely simple, of course. It is possible – and a good option for the actress – that Natasha is overplaying her upset in order to draw Andrei towards her. The play will certainly prove her brimful of cunning; but one of the most interesting things to watch in the theatre is a character changing, and her manipulativeness may only come out with time. Certainly it is important to see that at this moment she has been inconsiderately treated. As for her and Andrei's relationship, at this stage you can tell no more about it than you can from watching two people in life: the usual complex private mechanisms are at work. It is surprising, from what we have seen of Natasha so far, that Andrei should be so stricken by her; but there's no accounting for taste, and it may be that his chosen means of escape is someone quite unable to help him.

Natasha wastes no time in implicitly accepting his proposal with an embrace, much to the surprise of 'two officers' who happen to come into the drawing room. They are not named, and may be newcomers from outside. In practice, they are more likely to be Fedotik and Rodé, who have perhaps left the table during the business of the top and the photograph. (For most theatre managements two new silent characters mean a waste of resources, though the text does call for two non-speaking officers in Act Four as well.) Whoever they are, a proposal of marriage makes a good moment on which to close the scene, and it is rendered comic by the device of an interrupted or observed kiss. The spring is set for Act Two.

Act Two

By the beginning of the second act, Andrei and Natasha are man and wife and have a small son, Bobik; the setting is exactly the same but the atmosphere utterly changed. It is eight o'clock on a late winter's evening and the room is unlit: instead of Andrei's violin as in the old days, the only music to be heard is the rougher sound of an accordion from the street outside. If Act One ended in bright sunlight, in a mixture of hopefulness and comedy, there are now long shadows, only dispelled a little as Natasha now crosses the stage with a candle, checking that all unnecessary lights are out and establishing what Andrei is doing this particular evening.

Her question as to whether he is reading, though it seems unimportant to her, is enough to bring Andrei from his study with a book. He uses the affectionate version of his wife's name, Natasha, but his tone is very different from the ecstatic speech ('I love you, I love you as I've never loved anyone') of – in stage terms – a few moments ago:

> What is it, Natasha?

As it turns out, her preoccupations are domestic: a carnival party will soon be arriving, and the inattentive servants have to be watched carefully, she says. This might be fair enough, but her attitude sounds strict – last night there was a candle left alight at midnight and:

> I still haven't found out who lit it.

Clearly this is no longer the shy and awkward girl worried about her teasing reception by her future in-laws and friends. She seems to see herself as head of the household, with only limited sympathy for her husband and his sisters, entitled to discipline and punish the servants as she chooses – something it is hard to imagine the more relaxed Prozorov sisters doing. As for them, she notes that Olga and Irina are late home:

Olga's fatiguing work gets a mention, and as for Irina, who now appears to be working at the telegraph office, she gets a little perfunctory sympathy too:

> I said that to your sister this morning. 'You must look after yourself, Irina darling', I said. But she doesn't listen.

Natasha seems more worried about Bobik's health – a fever yesterday and 'freezing' today. Andrei says virtually nothing to this beyond mild reassurance – he sounds more fatigued than affectionate:

> He's fine, Natasha. The boy's fine.
> NATASHA: Still, we'd better see he's eating properly.

There is some sense of a well-worn routine – the husband half listening as the wife goes on and on.

We can see that one of Natasha's ways of dealing with contradiction is to change the subject. It would be better if tonight's carnival party were cancelled, she feels; and Andrei's reasonable point that the revellers have actually been invited is met by:

> You know, that darling little boy woke up this morning and looked at me, and he suddenly smiled – yes, he recognised me.

She then makes the doting point that children like Bobik 'understand perfectly', as if he were already her little ally. Then, having circled round it for a moment, she is back on her main intention: the visitors must be sent away. This is quite a decision: this carnival party was part of the very old and popular Russian festival of *maslenitsa* (the equivalent of Mardi Gras or Shrove Tuesday), when mummers would visit the villages. There would be feasting and bonfires and a scarecrow might be burned to celebrate the death of winter and beginning of spring. Andrei demurs again:

> Well, surely that's up to my sisters. I mean, it's their house.

– but he is overruled. This time Natasha purposely misunderstands, as if Andrei had said it was simply a matter of the girls being informed of her decision:

Yes, of course, I'll tell them too. They're so kind.

Then she changes the subject again; first to something new, a reminder that Andrei is not the man he could be:

I've ordered sour milk for supper. The doctor says you're to have nothing but sour milk, otherwise you'll never lose weight.

– and then to a more important point, which Andrei may have sensed her working up to. Her proposal is that the sickly Bobik should move into Irina's bedroom, which is:

dry, and gets the sun all day. She'll have to be told, and she can move in with Olga meantime . . .

Again, from Natasha, the imperative tone – 'she'll have to be told' – and a remarkable self-assurance. And so Irina will have to come home after her day's labours to share a room with her elder sister, as though they were visitors in a house with insufficient accommodation, while Bobik will have almost more space than he needs. Natasha's strategies are quick and would keep anyone on their toes. A moment ago she expressed a modicum of sympathy for the industrious Olga, but now she almost accuses her of domestic absenteeism:

She's not at home during the day anyway, she's only here at nights . . .

In response, Andrei is notably weak-willed:

A pause.
NATASHA: Andryusha, love, you're not answering.
ANDREI: I'm thinking . . . Anyway, I've nothing to say . . .

Natasha at last remembers something to do with someone other than herself and Bobik – the practical fact that Ferapont (last seen bringing in Protopopov's cake) has been waiting for some time to see Andrei. In fact Ferapont will soon make clear that he has been there since before dusk, but:

. . . they wouldn't let me in, no. The master's busy, they said.

Presumably this delay was Natasha's doing; Andrei does not seem particularly busy. It is also hard to know why the old man should have been left in the street, as suggested by the precise stage direction that he is in an 'old, shabby overcoat, with the collar turned up, and a scarf round his ears'. He has brought with him a book of some kind from Protopopov, together with a package of documents – from which we learn that Andrei, far from progressing in the academic world, now works for the regional council.

Andrei seems disproportionately pleased to see Ferapont; but he is, after all, someone to talk to – and by the same token Andrei is looking forward to going into his office the next day:

> . . . Tomorrow's Friday, there's no meeting, but I'll go in anyway . . . it'll give me something to do, I'm bored stiff at home . . .

So this, bluntly, is his position: marriage, fatherhood and home are giving him less and less pleasure, and he has sacrificed his intellectual prospects for a mundane job and domestic unhappiness. Now he admits as much, though he might not speak so bluntly if it were not for the fact that Ferapont is hard of hearing. Throughout the play Andrei will speak to the old man with this freedom – it is Chekhov's adroit method of letting him open his heart to us, the audience.

Andrei confirms what we must be suspecting. He still dreams of being a Professor at Moscow University, famous throughout Russia, but here he is, secretary of the council, hoping for promotion and working under a boss, Protopopov, whom the family is scornful of. It should be said that the regional council, or *zemstvo*, had been founded as an instrument of democratic local government within Chekhov's lifetime, in 1864. It would have been particularly approved of by Chekhov since it made it possible for doctors such as himself to provide free medical services, and its work would, in theory at least, have appealed to a liberal intellectual such as Andrei. However, by the turn of the century, when the play is set, its limitations were becoming painfully apparent, and Andrei's experience of it seems to be of daily drudgery.

In addition, his wife doesn't understand him, and as for talking to his sisters:

> I'm afraid they'll laugh at me, or make me feel ashamed.

His dream of escape is at least as self-indulgent as theirs:

> what wouldn't I give to be sitting right now in Moscow at Tyestov's, or the Grand Hotel!

– not so much for the food and drink perhaps, as just for the sake of being there.

Chekhov is careful to debunk Andrei's dreams, as he does those of his sisters, with comedy. As can be the way with deaf people, connection comes and goes for Ferapont: he sometimes catches nothing, at others the general drift, but there is one magic word he never misses – Moscow. This time it reminds him of a story he heard from a builder, that a certain merchant, perhaps in a competition, ate forty or maybe fifty pancakes there and then dropped dead.

Andrei seems to be as deaf to this interesting anecdote as Ferapont was to Andrei, and he elaborates his dream. It is the fantasy of a lonely man who would like to shed his solitude without troubling to make actual contact with anyone else:

> Yes, you can sit in Moscow, in an enormous restaurant dining room, you don't know anybody, nobody knows you, and yet you don't feel like a stranger.

Here, on the other hand, everybody knows him but he feels all the more alienated and estranged. Ferapont doesn't get any of this:

> What?
> *A pause*

– but has another bizarre story up his sleeve: the same lively builder told him there was a rope stretched right across Moscow, from one end to the other. This improbability arrests Andrei's attention – what would it be for? Ferapont has no explanation:

I dunno. That's what the builder said.

The bleak comedy of this is that the two men seem as far apart as if not one but both were deaf – and when, a moment later, Ferapont departs, Andrei is so little aware of it that he continues inviting him to leave the room after he has gone:

FERAPONT: Shall I go?
ANDREI: You can go now. Take care, old chap.
Ferapont exits.
Take care. (*Reading.*) You can come back tomorrow, collect these papers . . . Off you go.
A pause.
He's gone.
The door-bell rings.
Yes, more work . . . (*Stretches, and makes his way to his own room.*)

However, before the old man went there was a wonderfully revealing moment. Andrei asked him if he had ever been to Moscow, about which he has so much to say. For an old peasant in the provinces, that would certainly be very unlikely; and Ferapont replied, without protest or humour, but with a certain dignity:

I haven't. It's not been God's will.

Since much of the play resounds with upper-class people complaining about not getting to Moscow – when, technically, they have the means to do so – Ferapont's stoical recognition that certain things are out of his reach (a limitation he patiently attributes to God), should be particularly moving. Perhaps the family could learn a lesson from him.

*

The opening exchange of the act between Natasha and Andrei has dramatically underlined for us the passage of time and the deterioration in a relationship which had looked so promising, at least to them. In fact it was hardly an exchange at all: it is very clear who now wears the trousers, and how little Natasha is challenged. The scene could be staged with Andrei as its still point in the centre, weakly seated, or off to the side – it doesn't really matter; the important thing is to see how he uses his book. This is sometimes called a 'shadow move' – a physical detail that reveals a state of mind. Andrei's determined absorption in it shows not only how uninterested he really is in Natasha but how much he wants to avoid engaging at all, even at moments when he really should, such as when his sisters are affected. You might call it cowardice; it is certainly a measure of his inability to cope with his wife. From such a small detail we can see that her control over him and the household is indeed awesome.

Meanwhile the picture building up of Natasha is certainly not very attractive – she is punitive towards negligent servants, obsessed with small things, careless of everyone's needs but those of her baby. But it is important for the actress, and therefore for the audience, to keep this in proportion. For one thing, though it may seem hard on Irina, the change of room that Natasha proposes (only temporarily, she says) may be quite sensible: in that place, at that time, a sick baby could die if not kept warm and comfortable. Soon enough it will be difficult to sympathise with Natasha at all; but at this stage we should at least see her point of view and notice how little Andrei does to moderate it. After all, a partner in any relationship can only become this domineering if they are implicitly allowed to be by the other.

In all his scenes with his wife, Andrei could be played in a number of ways – henpecked and mutely submissive, or ill-humoured with moments of rebellion – but what outbursts he manages seem weak. Much of the time he seems unwilling to stand up for himself at all. Clearly the marriage has not brought the whole family together, and within Andrei's escapist dream of Moscow may be a sense of guilt that he has failed to arbitrate between his determined wife and his uneasy sisters. We may certainly wonder whether this man – so mild with Natasha, so confidential with a deaf man – is doing as much as he could for the good of the household he has helped to form.

*

Two by two, the larger company now begins to assemble, the atmosphere influenced by the sound of Anfisa singing Bobik to sleep somewhere offstage. Natasha seems to have accepted that illumination is now needed in the house, and so a maid appears as well to light an oil-lamp and candles, while Vershinin and Masha arrive in conversation. The sound-effect of the lullaby gently counterpoints the talk, as Andrei's violin did in the first act. Masha and Vershinin may be arriving from dinner somewhere inside the house or merely drifting in from a rather unseasonal walk outside. Certainly, the onstage room used for lunch in the last act seems not to be occupied, and the somewhat gloomy state of the house – meals here generally seem to be quite lively affairs – suggests it is relatively empty.

Despite the lapse of time, the pattern of the first act is about to be repeated, but in more sombre colours. The place is the same, and so is the general tendency to talk, especially to compare the past and the future with the present. Masha sounds unhurried, coming to the point slowly, feeling her way towards an opinion:

> I don't know.
> *A pause.*
> I don't know.

It sounds as if they have been talking about the good old days, and she admits that her feelings about them may be unreliable:

> Habit counts for a good deal, of course, what you're accustomed to. After father's death, for example, we just couldn't get used to the fact that we didn't have orderlies any longer.

What she does feel 'justified in saying', though, is that the military, as represented here by Vershinin, are 'the most decent, the most honourable and well-bred' people in the town. It is a cautious judgment – she also admits that the town itself may be untypical – but a flattering one for Vershinin to hear, since she has clearly thought carefully about it. He, however, seems oblivious to the compliment:

> I'm really thirsty. I wouldn't mind some tea.

Now Masha subtly compares her husband with him, and her
ease with Vershinin suggests that their relationship has moved
on since the day when she bluntly failed to recognise him. And
she seems eager to confirm to him Irina's earlier account of
her marriage to Kulygin. She was eighteen and had only just
left school when she met him, she explains, and such a teacher
was still impressive to her:

> He was terribly learned, clever and important, so I thought.

– but not any more. Vershinin is diplomatic:

> Yes . . . I see.

As if to match his politeness, she rather unconvincingly exon-
erates Kulygin from her next complaint:

> I'm not talking about my husband, I've got used to him,
> but among civilians in general there are so many boorish
> people, no manners, badly brought up. It upsets me,
> rudeness really offends me . . .

There is a vein of snobbishness here, as in her lament about
having to do without orderlies: and as for rudeness, she is
capable of it herself but too thin-skinned to take it in return.
Perhaps, after all, she is making her point to draw the subject
back to her husband:

> when people show a lack of sensitivity, or kindness, or
> common courtesy, I feel pain. When I'm with the teachers,
> for instance, my husband's colleagues, I really suffer.

Vershinin, who has listened non-committally, ventures to
disagree, or at least to say the case is not proved: it seems to
him that soldiers and civilians are 'pretty much of a much-
ness'. No, he feels the problem is a broader Russian one:
anyone who can think at all is fed up with their marriage or
their home, even 'sick to death of their horses'. How can such
petty responses to life run side by side with a Russian's intellectual ambition? Why is that? The interrogative word swings
to and fro between him and Masha, almost playfully, emphasising the new easiness between them:

MASHA: Why?
VERSHININ: Why is your average Russian sick to death of his wife and children? And why are his wife and children sick of him?

Wife and children – Vershinin is veering towards his favourite subject. His gloominess is unusual, Masha feels, and not very becoming:

You're not at your best today.

Softly rebuked in this way, he blames his mood on hunger, just as he just blamed it on thirst. But it's clear what is really on his mind: one of his daughters is sick, he had a two-hour row with his wife today, starting at seven in the morning, and he is fretful that the girls have such a bad mother. We might notice that it is now evening; his not having troubled to go back during the last twelve hours can't have helped. Instead here he is with Masha, more and more drawn to her as the only woman who can understand his predicament. The emotion of the day allows him to declare himself to her. Kissing her hand, he says something comically untrue:

I never talk about these things . . .

Having been watching them, we may also not agree that:

it's strange I should be telling you.

Masha can hardly miss the meaning of it, either way. She evades; it may be unwelcome, but more probably she is sensitive to the overture but wants to put Vershinin off for now. She is a married woman in a very small community, after all. As people will, she immediately talks about something else, though what she chooses creates an image almost as ominous as their developing feelings:

The stove's making such a noise. The chimney howled just like that just before Father died.

Vershinin, ever the realist, is entertained that she is superstitious enough to think of such a thing, and it doesn't deter him:

What a magnificent, wonderful creature you are. Truly magnificent and wonderful! It's dark in here, yet I can still see your eyes shining.

Her next reaction is as true to life as her change of subject was:

(*Sits down in another chair.*) It's lighter over here . . .

She likes his attention more and more, particularly now he has so emphatically come to the point::

VERSHININ: I love you, I love you . . . I love your eyes, your every movement, I dream about them . . . A magnificent, wonderful woman!
MASHA (*softly laughing*): When you speak to me like that, I laugh, I don't know why, even though I'm terrified.

However her enjoyment is compromised by conscience and propriety:

Please, don't say it again . . . (*Barely audible.*) No, go on, say it, I don't mind . . . (*Covers her face with her hands.*) It doesn't matter. There's someone coming . . .

Just as well. All the ingredients of the secretly developing relationship are evident. Adultery was a criminal offence in Russia then – a crime against society and not just a private matter – so there is anxiety here, excitement, a sense of bad omen.

Irina and Tuzenbakh, also in mid-conversation, now approach Vershinin and Masha through the upstage ballroom, but do not see them at first. Tuzenbakh is repeating something that seems to obsess him a little. Having insisted in the first act, in the midst of his philosophising, that he really is a Russian, he now reiterates that despite his German name (which we now get in triple-barrelled glory, 'Tuzenbakh-Krone-Altschauer') he is an orthodox Russian like the rest of them. At least he seems able to turn it into a joke this time rather than an excuse for excessive emotion – the only thing German left in him is:

the way I keep pestering you, walking you home every evening.

He will go on, in fact, until she sends him away, something he expects sooner than a return of his devotion.

So this walk home is a nightly occurrence. Irina's reply may not be meant unkindly, but it is certainly unresponsive:

> Oh, I'm worn out!

In the first act, though she never pretended to love him, she usually answered him freshly and briskly. Now she prefers to deflect, and may be glad to find someone else to talk to. So she tells Masha about an incident at the telegraph office where she works:

> You know, a woman came in just now, she was sending a telegram to her brother in Saratov . . .

It transpires that her exhaustion involves a sense of shame: this customer was bereaved, trying to cable her brother to let him know that her son had died, and Irina was unaccountably rude to her because she couldn't remember his address. In the end the telegram had to be addressed hopelessly just 'to Saratov'. Irina's treatment of the unfortunate woman certainly seems rough:

> 'I haven't got all day', I said. It was really stupid of me.

That seems to be all she has in her for the moment. She is neither cheered nor further depressed by the possibility that the carnival musicians are on their way; no, above all:

> I need a rest. I'm exhausted.

Tuzenbakh keeps going, though his form of words is unlikely to cheer her up – especially coming so soon after Vershinin's splendid wooing of Masha:

> Every time you come in from work you look such a pathetic little thing . . .
> *A pause.*

It might not be quite what any woman wants to hear – at any rate, she says for the third time:

I'm tired . . .

The two of them seem to have settled into a pattern: Tuzenbakh keeps professing love; she, out of sorts in one way or another, avoids it. Her longing for work, partly fired up by him, has led her to this: a tiring and meaningless job with 'no poetry'. But her dreams of Moscow persist, and they are quite precise:

> We'll be moving there in June, and between now and June there's still . . . February, March, April, May . . . almost six months!

Some more information follows: Andrei has been gambling, regularly losing money since December. This is obviously alarming for his family, though Irina manages perversely to turn it into a wish:

> I wish he'd lose everything, then perhaps we'd be able to get away from this town.

This is the old Irina, casting realism to the winds for the sake of fantasy. But a sharper side of her comes out when Masha hopes that Natasha (who should be as concerned as they are about dwindling fortunes, especially with a new baby) doesn't find out about it:

> I don't think she cares.

This remark, which may not be fair, implies that Natasha expects to be provided for come what may, regardless of any difficulties.

Lest the scene become too weighed down with information, Chekhov begins to allow inconsequential life to seep in at its sides. The fact that a carnival party is expected may be the reason all the officers have gathered at the house this evening. Just as someone knocked from downstairs to attract Chebutykin's attention in the first act, he himself now knocks, a sign that he wants to come up, and Tuzenbakh's returning knock authorises him: in a moment he is here, again with his newspaper. Then another unsettling hint about the Prozorovs' circumstances is dropped. We learn that Chebutykin is their lodger, but that he hasn't paid his rent for eight months. Still more important, Irina and Masha seem unconcerned:

> IRINA: . . . It's obviously slipped his mind.
> MASHA *(laughs)*: And sitting there, so self-importantly.

It is as if these sisters aren't expected to be diligent about such things, even though the brother, who is, gambles away their money and their sister-in-law doesn't care. In the lightest way, Chekhov suggests that they are set on a blind and disastrous course.

Vershinin's need continues to be for tea; Chebutykin requires Irina's help (or company) as he lays out a game of patience. The slightly comic effect of the officers' taste for philosophy is emphasised when Vershinin turns to it for lack of anything more comforting:

> Oh well, if they won't give us any tea, then at least we can have a discussion.

It is as if a good talk about life will at least prevent them all slipping off to sleep. What follows, like so much else in the act, runs parallel to what happened in the first, but in this case at much greater length. On that occasion, the discussion between Vershinin and Tuzenbakh never really got going, partly because of Vershinin's interest in his female audience. What happens now is more sustained – five minutes or so of stage time – and the punctuations are more numerous and subtle. For instance, as Vershinin warms to his theme, Masha, newly pleased with him, again 'laughs softly'; when he speaks of the happiness that may be the lot of his grandchildren, the two younger officers, Fedotik and Rodé, come in and sing quietly to the guitar; soon Masha again 'laughs softly'. Ongoing throughout is the gentle activity of Irina and Chebutykin over their cards; and pauses are specified by Chekhov, either to let the argument sink in or to allow these incidental sights and sounds to register. Most tellingly, when Tuzenbakh, unusually concise, responds to Vershinin's need for 'meaning' in life:

> Meaning? . . . Look, it's snowing. What does that mean?

– there is a pause. Almost immediately, there is another, after Masha enters the conversation to summarise what Vershinin has said and to align herself with him:

> I think people should believe in something . . . To live without knowing why cranes fly, or why children are born, or why there are stars in the sky . . . I mean, you either know why you're alive, or else it's all just nonsense, absolutely pointless . . .

It is interesting to notice how the positions of Vershinin and Tuzenbakh have shifted a little. When he first arrived, Vershinin's view was that the life they were living would come to seem 'trivial . . . bizarre and uncomfortable . . . none too clean, maybe even sinful'; while Tuzenbakh, insofar as he made any headway, believed that they would be respected by future generations because of the relative progress they have made. Once again, both are looking to the future. Vershinin feels that in two or three hundred years, 'or a thousand, say', 'a new happy life' will have dawned, and the entire purpose of the present is to work towards it, suffer and prepare for it. Tuzenbakh counters that for all the future's marvellous new practical inventions, life will be much the same – 'people'll still be sighing, "God, what a life".' But he views this with irony, not pessimism; after all, in his dogged and devoted way, he is happy now – 'How am I to convince you?'

During this, Vershinin makes a confession about his intellectual limits. He went to the same Cadet School as Tuzenbakh, but didn't go on to the Academy, and his lack of further education means that, although an eager reader, he has:

> no idea how to choose books, and possibly I don't read the things I should.

Quite endearingly, he feels his life passing, his hair going grey:

> and yet I understand so little – so very little.

Tuzenbakh is noticeably wittier than before – he imagines for the future the flight of balloons, some 'new fashion in men's jackets', the discovery of a sixth sense; and his clarity about nature's indifference to men's theories is beautifully expressed:

> Take migrating birds, for instance, like cranes – they keep
> on flying . . . without knowing why or where to. They'll
> keep flying, supposing all manner of thinkers were to
> spring up amongst them. They can think all they want, as
> long as they keep flying . . .

His repetition of 'flying' might cause the company to look out at the window at the snow and the Russian steppe rolling away, as far across the Siberian east as westward towards Moscow. Never in the play has it seemed so far away; and Masha decides enough is enough:

> MASHA: As Gogol says, 'Life is a bore, my friends!'
> TUZENBAKH: Yes, and I say it's hard work arguing with
> you, my friends! I give up . . .

*

Half way through this long central movement of the act, with the stage filling up, the technical challenge in practice is as it was in Act One: everyone has to be visible when they speak and if possible when they are not. Chebutykin, Fedotik and Rodé, less important so far, can slip in discreetly. But every new arrival significant to the plot – Vershinin with Masha, Tuzenbakh with Irina – has to be able to attract the audience's attention by being strongly positioned before partially retreating to a less prominent part of the stage.

The key to what Chekhov is up to here – and a most important thing for the director and actors to deal with – is his use of the evident development in the central relationships to carry his story forward, whilst also suggesting the passage of time. To be technical: Irina referred to June being nearly six months away, so this is January (a little early for *maslenitsa*). The first act took place in May, and so if this is the beginning of the following year, Natasha must have been pregnant when we first met her with Andrei. If, on the other hand, Bobik was conceived in wedlock, there must be twenty months between Act One and a January for Act Two, allowing him to be nearly a year old. However, the audience doesn't really have the leisure to do these calculations as they watch. Instead, they observe how Vershinin and Masha, Tuzenbakh and Irina, and of course Andrei and Natasha have changed – a far more effective way of suggesting the lapse of time than any bald announcement of how great it is. Chekhov achieves this all the better because he is closely following the pattern of the first act, when individuals or pairs gradually arrived until the stage was full; we instinctively remember this and therefore notice more easily what has changed and what has not.

For instance, Masha and Vershinin are now allowed to be alone together; they are at ease and talk in a relaxed way, despite the implicit energy beneath the surface. At the same time, when Vershinin does declare his love, it is entirely up to the director and actors to decide whether he has done it before or not – there is no evidence. The relationship between Tuzenbakh and Irina, following them on, seems to have developed as well, but more in the way of habit than intensification – Tuzenbakh as loyal as ever, but Irina more tired.

As always, Vershinin seems sincere and eloquent, but we cannot be altogether sure that the vulnerable Masha is safe to trust him. As he philosophises with Tuzenbakh, both men's arguments have more charm than before, and feel more personal, as if they have had many such talks in the intervening months. Tuzenbakh in particular is more humorous and even quite terse on occasion.

*

There seems to be an instinctive agreement to lighten up the talk. Chebutykin discovers what is to him an interesting fact: the French writer Balzac was married in the Russian town of Berdichev. He decides to make a note of it: it is another diverting titbit to replace real intellectual activity. Irina, softly singing, lays out another round of patience and repeats Chebutykin's discovery in a murmur. It's as if anyone can say anything, and it doesn't matter very much if it makes sense – even though a few moments ago presenting a persuasive argument and being understood was all-important. Tuzenbakh, less able to get off his pet themes than the rest, turns to Masha to give her the news that he is retiring from the army (it is not clear whether Irina knows this), largely so that he can:

work one day in my life, come home at night and collapse
onto the bed exhausted, fall asleep on the spot.

– and he wanders off into the ballroom with an observation
that no actual hard-working man would be likely to take
pleasure in:

Yes, working people sleep soundly, I should imagine.

The congenial chat continues, an apparently random drift that
is, as ever, cunningly orchestrated. Fedotik gives Irina some
coloured pencils he has bought her, and her mixture of
precociousness and innocence is beautifully expressed:

You've got so used to treating me like a child, but I'm
a grown woman . . . (*Accepts the pencils and penknife,
delightedly.*) Oh, these are lovely!

Rodé asks the Doctor his age – loudly; Chebutykin responds
with the charming lie that he's thirty-two; Fedotik offers to
show Irina a different kind of patience; the samovar is brought
in and Natasha arrives and 'busies herself at the table'.
Soliony, awkward as ever, enters alone and greets everyone –
an unnecessary formality; Vershinin comments on the sound
of the wind outside; and Masha declares herself sick of
winter. Irina takes her success at patience to mean they will go
to Moscow, but she is wrong – Fedotik points out she has
made a mistake in the game, so once again the sisters' dearest
wish is subtly discredited. Chebutykin comments on a small-
pox epidemic. We know that something will develop soon, like
a theme of music emerging from the tuning-up of an orche-
stra, but in the meanwhile time seems simply to be passing at
its own pace.

For a moment something definite seems to be coming through
when Natasha addresses the assembled company about Bobik,
as she is always inclined to do, though their interest in the
child must be limited to the polite. The 'special way' he looks
at her, his mother, proves to her how extraordinary he is. Her
boastfulness (compared with Tuzenbakh's recent denigration
of himself as a soldier) is jarring; and though the others might
not choose to be so outrageous, they may have a sneaking
sympathy with Soliony's declaration:

Yes, well, if that child was mine, I'd fry him up in a pan
and eat him.

He then stalks off with his drink and sits alone in a corner.
Natasha's protest:

Oh, what a rude, ignorant man!

– noticeably finds no sympathetic response, and Masha changes
the subject as if it were of no interest.

Masha feels that the real reason winter is having such a
depressing effect on her is that she is simply in the wrong
place. If she were in Moscow, she wouldn't notice such things.
It is her particular friend Vershinin who briskly disposes of
this delusion, delivering one of the the play's most telling
putdowns of the sisters' ambitions. He has recently read the
writings of an imprisoned government minister, who takes
special notice of the birds in the sky because he sees them out
of his cell window but cannot reach them: but he never
noticed them as a free man, and won't when he is free again.
Similarly, the sisters will take Moscow for granted once they
get there. Part of Vershinin's repertoire does seem to be to
blunt the Prozorovs' aspirations; here he is merciless, and quite
right perhaps to suggest that to travel hopefully is better than
to arrive. Still, it is a tough thing for Masha to hear from her
major admirer.

It seems that Soliony has eaten all the sweets, and this trivial
moment forms a bridge to a more important event. Anfisa,
having served everyone with tea in her usual way, brings
Vershinin an unusual message, a note from his daughter to say
that his wife has attempted suicide by poison. Or perhaps not
so unusual: Tuzenbakh mentioned this habit of hers when he
first introduced Vershinin, though Vershinin himself has not
specifically mentioned it till now.

> VERSHININ (*in a low voice*): I'm sorry, Masha, I've got to
> leave . . . My wife's taken poison again. I must go. I'll try
> and slip out unnoticed.

Because of the 'again' it's possible that the audience will laugh.
As for Masha, albeit he leaves with a great compliment to her:

My dearest darling, glorious Masha . . .

– her distress at his sudden departure comes out as destructiveness. She is hostile to the harmless Anfisa – 'Stop pestering me'; she messes up Irina's game of patience; and attacks the amused Chebutykin for talking 'damned nonsense' at his age. Into this one-woman hornet's nest, Natasha, oblivious, ventures:

> Masha, my dear . . . You shouldn't use such expressions, you really shouldn't . . . I mean, with your good looks you could be quite enchanting, honestly, even in the very best society, if it weren't for your language. *Je vous prie pardonnez-moi, Marie, mais vous avez des manières un peu grossières.*

Earlier in the nineteenth century, Russians would speak French to suggest superior breeding, emphasising their West European rather than Asian mentality; but by the time of the play it would have seemed highly affected.

The comedy is that, faced with such an affront, Masha, having just verbally turned the room topsy-turvy, is literally speechless. Meanwhile Natasha may notice Tuzenbakh's attempts to smother his amusement:

> Pass me that . . . pass me . . . I think that's the brandy.

– or perhaps not; she is certainly not deterred, and may even feel perversely encouraged. She embarks on another Gallicism, but her French is poor, inaccurately learned from a book. In what she now says, for instance, 'il me semble' would be much better than 'il paraît':

> *Il paraît que mon Bobik déjà ne dort pas*, he's wakened up.

Then she leaves to attend to him, her head presumably held high.

It is interesting that nobody says anything about this incident: the conversation immediately shifts to Vershinin's sudden departure and then to an attempt by Tuzenbakh to come to terms with the surly Soliony. It may be that nobody is quite sure what everyone else feels about Natasha, so that it would be risky to say something rude about her. But it is noticeable throughout the play that, much as the sisters complain about her among themselves, Natasha has the ability to reduce them to silence, paralysing them as effectively as a predator does its prey.

The peace-making Tuzenbakh is finding Soliony evasive and unhelpful at first, as he perhaps expected:

> SOLIONY: Why shouldn't we be friends? I've no quarrel with you.
> TUZENBAKH: No, but you always make me feel as if something's happened between us. You're a strange man, you must admit it.
> SOLIONY (*declaiming*): 'I am strange, yet who is not! Be not angry, Aleko!'
> TUZENBAKH: What's Aleko got to do with it?
> *A pause.*

Yes, indeed: the reference will be lost on a modern audience, but Tuzenbakh would get it. Aleko was the murdering hero of a poem by Alexander Pushkin, a young aristocrat who kills his gypsy wife and her lover. In fact this quote is not in the poem: Soliony is just using the ominous name to baffle him.

Over the brandy Tuzenbakh perseveres with his awkward colleague; and Soliony relents a little, offering a surprisingly candid assessment of his own character. He is best on his own, he explains, quite decent, more than averagely honourable; but in company he gets 'depressed, and withdrawn' and says 'all kinds of stupid things'. We might define such a thing as no more than chronic shyness; this clearly is a misfit and a solitary, whose misanthropy might well be compensating for social awkwardness.

Ever good-natured, Tuzenbakh seems to accept this, exchanging confidence for confidence: he finds Soliony irritating because of his constant teasing, but he has some affection for him too. Soliony withdraws a little into his pose: he has no personal grudge against Tuzenbakh, but is simply the victim of his own temperament, which he now compares to that of the great romantic poet Mikhail Lermontov:

(*Quietly.*) I even look a bit like Lermontov . . . so I've been
told . . . (*He takes a bottle of scent from his pocket and pours it
over his hands.*)

In his own peculiar way, in fact, he is warming up. Still, he
seems no more interested than anyone else in the Baron's
resolution to give up the army and do some useful work. When
Chebutykin drifts in from the farther room with Irina, fondly
remembering a meal he once had that featured a Caucasian
meat speciality, *chekhartma*, Soliony is ready for another skir-
mish. No, he says; *cheremsha* is not meat but a vegetable like an
onion, so Chebutykin must have been mistaken. The absurdity
here is that both are quite correct about the two different
words, and the joke depends on their not hearing – or not
choosing to hear – the difference in each other's pronun-
ciation. The argument is unresolved – Andrei stops it – and
disappears in a brief outburst of drunken dancing and singing
between Andrei, Chebutykin and Tuzenbakh, their spirits
raised by the imminent arrival of the carnival party. Soliony,
perhaps maddened by all the conviviality, finds a new opportunity to pick a quarrel:

> TUZENBAKH (*kisses Andrei*): . . . I'm coming with you, old
> chap, to Moscow, to the university.
> SOLIONY: Which one? There are two universities in Moscow.
> ANDREI: There's only one university in Moscow.
> SOLIONY: And I say there are two.
> ANDREI: Why not three? The more the merrier.
> SOLIONY: There are two universities in Moscow!

Again the argument is absurd, but more uncomfortable this
time: Soliony has picked not on a colleague but on one of his
hosts, a potential professor who could be expected to know the
facts about Moscow University. He also appears to be losing
his temper: if everyone insists on disagreeing with him like
this, it must mean they are not interested in his conversation.
So he stalks foolishly out of the room.

Tuzenbakh finds Soliony's sulk no more than amusing; he has
already declared his intention to get drunk tonight, and is
determined on a good time for all:

... let the dancing begin, I shall sit down to play! That
Soliony's so funny ... (*Sits at the piano, begins to play a
waltz.*)

Masha waltzes alone, improvising an obvious enough line:

The Baron's drunk, the Baron's drunk, the Baron's drunk!

But the company has not reckoned with little Bobik and
Natasha, who is on the warpath. Although she could hardly
make herself heard in the current revelry, she can whisper to
Chebutykin and then leave him to pass on her discreet message to Tuzenbakh at the piano. In this indirect way the word
gets out that the party must stop and the company disperse:

IRINA: What's the matter?
CHEBUTYKIN: It's time we were going. Good night all.
TUZENBAKH: Good night. Time to go.

It is left to Natasha's unfortunate husband to explain the
cancellation – all the harder for him, since he is the only one
who had advance warning that the carnival party was to be
sent away:

IRINA: What do you mean? What about the musicians?
ANDREI (*embarrassed*): There won't be any. The thing is, my
dear – you see, Natasha says Bobik's not too well, and
because of that ... Oh, I don't know – frankly, I don't care
either way.

It is not a great performance by Andrei. In any case, all
celebration, spontaneous or official, is off because of the
indisposition of the same Bobik who smiled in such a special
way at his mother, and whom Soliony would like to fry in a
pan.

Reactions to the disappointment are various. Irina is resigned
and neutral:

IRINA (*shrugs*): Bobik's not well ...

– but Masha is openly outraged, and surely puts much of the
company's feeling about Natasha into words:

> Oh, to hell with it! We're being thrown out, it seems, we've
> got to go. (*To Irina.*) It's not Bobik that's sick, it's her . . .
> Up here! (*Taps her forehead.*) Stupid woman!

This is embarrassing enough for Natasha's husband to leave
the room in silence. Without quite meaning it, Masha has also
prefigured the family's ultimate fate – 'We're being thrown
out, it seems . . . ' Of the junior officers, Rodé is as put out as
everyone else, but Fedotik – whose fairmindedness, it must be
said, contrasts rather well with the grumbling bias of everyone
else – is more tolerant:

> What a shame! I'd been looking forward to spending the
> evening here, but if the child's sick, well, of course . . . I'll
> bring him a toy tomorrow.

Chebutykin has slipped after Andrei into his study – for a
reason we will shortly learn. The rest of the party drift out
onto the wintry street, a Russian festivity looking for somewhere to happen. As their random calls die, the quiet sounds
of the house reassert themselves: Anfisa, singing, clears the
table and extinguishes the lights, and the stage is empty for a
moment.

*

Chekhov once said that 'people have dinner, that's all they do,
they have dinner; yet during this time their happiness is
established or their lives are falling apart'. He was an expert at
observing how strong emotions can be concealed behind commonplace activities – food, drink, banal chatter, cards, strains
of music – which paradoxically reveal the characters' inner
life. As this remarkably sustained company scene closes and
the stage drains of people, we remember how subjects started
up, began to develop, then stalled and died as they do in
life; the audience absorbed information about the characters'
relationships by eavesdropping on them rather than being
informed. Although little has been at stake, much was confirmed: Masha's connection with Vershinin, Natasha as the
cuckoo in the nest, Soliony the dark figure at the edge of the
group, Chebutykin and Tuzenbakh wanting to be close to

Irina – there are now several pots simmering on the stove, short of boiling point. Things almost came to a head when a party that might have become riotous and even quarrelsome (Bobik would indeed have had a bad night) was spoiled by Natasha, but apart from Masha's moment of outspokenness, nothing came of it and everyone simply drifted away with feelings of disappointment and flatness. Most deep feelings remained unspoken..

*

An oddly confidential connection, unnoticed before, seems to exist between Andrei and Chebutykin. Chebutykin's instinct to follow the younger man to his study a moment ago is explained now that they return, Andrei in his outdoor coat. They have thought of a solution. Their talk is exceptionally blunt, revealing Andrei's anger at his circumstances, and also an important hint about Chebutykin, the reason he never 'got round' to marrying:

> . . . life flashed past me, like lightning. Besides, I was madly in love with your dear mother, and she was already married . . .
> ANDREI: People shouldn't marry. They shouldn't, it's too boring.
> CHEBUTYKIN: Ah yes, but what about loneliness? You can dress it up any way you like, my dear chap, but loneliness is a terrible thing . . .

This is the second time Chebutykin has mentioned his attach-ment to Mrs Prozorov, and this time it is unambiguous. Their plan for temporary escape from their problems may be habitual:

> ANDREI: Let's be on our way.
> CHEBUTYKIN: What's the hurry? We've plenty of time.
> ANDREI: I don't want my wife stopping us.
> CHEBUTYKIN: Ah, I see.
> ANDREI: I won't play cards tonight, I'll just sit and watch.

Like a man dealing with alcohol addiction, Andrei is starting with the best intentions; no doubt Chebutykin gives him an old-fashioned 'look'. Andrei defensively changes the subject, paraphrasing a conversation that recurs in almost every play by this author. In a satirical comment on his own profession, Chekhov makes his fictional patient ask for help and get none:

> ANDREI: I'm not feeling too well . . . What should I do about shortness of breath, do you think?
> CHEBUTYKIN: Why ask me? I can't remember, dear boy, haven't a clue!

On which note, the doorbell rings (it is the carnival party) and they sneak off like two rogues.

Irina, who has arrived to learn from Anfisa who was at the door, is left alone, troubled – no doubt she feels there was no good reason to abandon the evening. The last person she would now wish to see is Soliony, but he is suddenly with her, having been sulking elsewhere in the house since his outburst. He is surprised but, as it turns out, pleased that everyone has gone. Apparently he wants to apologise for his behaviour, but in reality he has other things in mind. Irina quickly realises that he is taking advantage of the opportunity to profess love to her. Love is the constant refrain she hears from Tuzenbakh, whose loyal tenderness she may find a little dog-like; but it is preferable to Soliony's chilling elevation of her into something more than human:

> . . . you're not like the others. You're high above them, you're pure, you can see the truth . . . You're the only one who understands me. I love you, with a deep, everlasting . . . I can't live without you.

It is remarkably ill-judged. Why would Irina welcome the news that, compared to her, her closest friends and relatives are ignorant and impure? And the idea that only she understands him when there is little evidence that they have ever talked sounds like the oppressive language of the stalker. Not only that, but the promise that without her he will die is more a threat than a compliment. However, it is a threat directed not so much at her but at the harmless Tuzenbakh:

> . . . I won't tolerate a successful rival . . . I won't . . . I swear to you, by all that's holy, I'll kill any rival . . .

Like any human being, Soliony has a right to his dreams, if not to vengeance; and in fact it is not really clear if he is speaking from the heart or plagiarising the attitude of some romantic hero in Lermontov.

Irina has not given him an inch: the reverse of hospitable, she names his rank to emphasise the distance between them:

> Goodnight . . . Goodnight! Please leave . . . Captain
> Soliony, stop it.

His face is saved a little by the arrival of Natasha with her candle; despite his earlier insult she is at least polite to him, though in a somewhat simpering way:

> Oh, I beg your pardon, Captain, I didn't know you were
> here, I'm not properly dressed . . .

So he can get off with some of his considerable pride intact.

The act is now decelerating in a series of loosely-connected duologues, like tides flowing around Irina, who is an island of disappointment. She will find Natasha little more welcome than Soliony: her opinion of her is probably as strong as Masha's though less overt. Much as it was when she spoke of Irina's health to Andrei at the beginning of the act, Natasha's concern for her is questionable – she is about to change her accommodation, which she must know will be unwelcome. As ever, she sounds a little patronising:

> Oh, my poor dear girl, you look so tired! (*Kisses Irina.*) You
> really should go to bed earlier.

To escape, Irina enquires after Bobik, who has, unknowingly, caused the breakdown of the party. If he was poorly before, he seems to have improved:

> IRINA: Is Bobik asleep?
> NATASHA: Yes, he's sleeping. But he's a little restless.

Then comes the punch – the nursery is too cold and damp for a baby: it will be better if Irina moves in with Olga and Bobik has Irina's room.

Chekhov's mastery of this moment is to give Irina not an angry or shocked response but bafflement, which he then counterpoints with a distracting noise outside:

> IRINA (*uncomprehending*): Move where?
> *The sound of a troika, with bells jingling, drawing up outside.*

Natasha repeats her suggestion, attempting to seal the deal with her story of the baby's specialness: Irina should understand that Bobik is a 'sweet little thing', and that when Natasha speaks to him, he (unsurprisingly) looks up at her 'with his darling little eyes'.

Still Irina cannot absorb the news or reply before the doorbell rings. Presumably this is Olga, the absentee tonight, kept at work until late. In fact it is a surprise: Protopopov, Andrei's superior, has called to see if his wife would care to come for a ride. The message is sufficiently discreet for the maid to have to whisper it in Natasha's ear, so the audience is immediately alert to what kind of complication this might mean for the story:

> NATASHA (*laughs*): Really, men are so funny!

So, despite her worry about Bobik that necessitated cancelling the party, she will indeed:

> . . . go for a spin, just a quarter of an hour or so . . .

One wonders what Masha would have to say about this; but as Natasha hurries off to her assignation, Irina remains silently seated, 'deep in thought'. The two schoolteachers, Kulygin and Olga, arrive, followed by Vershinin, who has obviously wasted little time with his suicidal wife before returning. The men are of course taken aback at the lack of a party, and Irina is uncommunicative about the reason. Kulygin in particular sounds suspicious of Protopopov's presence outside, as if he were in some way threatened by it:

> . . . why's Protopopov waiting outside with his troika?
> Who's he waiting for?

Once again, Protopopov gets no patronymic.

Each of them reflects, in parallel, on their own troubles: Olga, who has been deputising for the headmistress, has a splitting headache – and what's more, Andrei's intention not to gamble with Chebutykin tonight is put into context. He lost two hundred roubles at cards last night, a very large sum, and it is the talk of the town. Kulygin doesn't seem to be interested in this:

> Yes, I felt tired at the meeting too.

– and as for Vershinin, his visit to his wife has confirmed his worst feelings about her. The abandoned woman:

> took it into her head to give me a fright just now – tried to poison herself. Still, it's all over now, I can relax . . .

He wants to stay out, and he wants company; even Kulygin, the husband of his 'glorious' Masha, will do for the purpose:

> Come on, my dear chap, let's go on somewhere – I can't stay at home, I simply can't.

But Kulygin is too cautious to do such a thing. He is tired, and curious about his wife's whereabouts – perhaps especially so in view of the ominous Protopopov, whom he vaguely senses as a transgressor. If he did but know it, his real rival is standing beside him. He talks of Masha not by name, but proprietorially:

> KULYGIN: Has my wife gone home?
> IRINA: I think so.

Reassured, he looks forward to two free days, and heads home, leaving a typical parting gift:

> *o, fallacem hominum spem!* Accusative case of exclamation . . .

Vershinin goes too, whistling like a man with few cares, and the two sisters are alone.

The act seems about to close at last. Olga is on her way to bed and Kulygin home; Vershinin is out on the town; Andrei and Chebutykin are gambling; Tuzenbakh, Masha, Fedotik and

Rodé have probably found nowhere to go and dispersed. Someone is playing the concertina outside; Soliony has gone like a bad dream; the house seems to be reclaiming its night's routine. As she clears the table and puts out the lights, Anfisa, like the soul of the house, is gently singing. Then at the last moment, Chekhov suddenly moves the atmosphere into a major key: Natasha typically jolts the prevailing mood, this time in fur coat and hat with her accomplice the maid, on her way to Protopopov, not so much for a quarter but 'about half an hour'. The bubble bursts: Irina, who has carried most of the burdens of the past few minutes, is left alone to dream, and she breathes it out:

(*With intense longing.*) To Moscow! Moscow! Moscow!

Chekhov's orchestration of the final moments of this act is the first of several superb diminuendoes that he achieves both in this play and *The Cherry Orchard*, which he wrote next. Olga's last speech gently repeats, like a refrain, things already said: her headache, Andrei's losses, the fact of two days' holiday. A steady musical decay is being punctuated by the unpredictable rhythms of life – whistling and quiet singing, the putting on of coats, an accordion playing in the street. It is so masterly that really a director in the theatre has only to do what the author tells him, and it will work.

Act Three

Although there is evidence that the original Moscow Art Theatre practice was to have quite lengthy pauses between each act, in the modern theatre there will most likely have been a single interval at this halfway point in the play. The returning audience may get the impression that they are now looking at the consequence of Natasha's plan to move Irina in with Olga. The downstairs drawing room and ballroom are gone; instead we see sleeping quarters, with beds perhaps partially visible behind the two screens on either side of the stage. But for some reason Masha is lying in her usual black clothes on the divan in front of them and no one else is there; her presence, and the sound of a distant fire alarm in what is clearly nighttime, warns us of something unusual. Masha, it turns out, is not the only one awake: she is immediately joined by Olga and old Anfisa, who is explaining that there are people in their night clothes outside in the yard, and some at the bottom of the stairs whom she has been trying to encourage up:

> . . . they're crying, 'We don't know where our Papa is', they say, 'Please God he hasn't died in the fire.'

The first children we will think of are Vershinin's, worried by their father's absence, though there must be many other candidates as well.

Alerted, the audience starts picking up a series of unexpected facts, and in all the bustle the actors must make sure they receive them clearly. The house, which is probably grander than most others in the town, is open to anyone whose home has been damaged: the fire has been extensive. Olga is now at the bedroom cupboard, pulling out dresses and giving them to Anfisa to distribute to the victims of the 'dreadful business':

> Kirsanov Street's burnt to the ground, it seems . . . and take this . . . and this . . . (*Flinging a dress into her arms.*) The

> Vershinins got a terrible fright, the poor things . . . Their
> house only just escaped. They can spend the night here . . .

The mention of his name suggests that it was indeed
Vershinin's children that Anfisa meant. The old nanny is too
heavily burdened now, and needs help, even if only from the
equally aged Ferapont. But Olga is doubtful if in the general
din he will hear the bell used to summon him – or indeed if
anyone else downstairs who could get the deaf old man moving will either. She goes out onto the landing to call, giving us
the opportunity to see a window there 'glowing red from the
fire', while a fire engine is heard noisily passing the house.

Whatever dramatic external events have shattered the calm of
this introverted household, Masha is still lying on the divan,
and there is no sign as yet of Irina or Natasha or Andrei. Olga,
frequently tired anyway, is bearing the brunt of the relief
effort. But Ferapont arrives surprisingly quickly to fulfil one
of his roles by putting the distance between here and Moscow
into a semi-comic context. His contribution to the present
crisis is another anecdote, this time about the 1812 assault on
Moscow by Napoleon's army:

> Yes, there was a fire in Moscow, too, in 1812. By God, the
> Frenchies didn't half get a fright!

In response, Olga bustles him downstairs with an armful of
clothes. In these topsy-turvy circumstances, even though she is:

> so tired, I can scarcely stand . . .

– provision must be made for everyone, indoors and out. Her
plan is this: Vershinin's two daughters can sleep in the
drawing-room we were in for the first two acts, Vershinin
himself and Tuzenbakh can also be 'downstairs' somewhere,
as will Fedotik – perhaps in the ballroom that was upstage of
the drawing room. On top of every other problem, there is one
bad reason for the shortage of space – Chebutykin, though
professionally equipped to help, has reacted to the disaster by
creating more:

> OLGA: The Doctor's drunk - it's as if he did it on purpose –
> he's terribly drunk, we can't put anyone in with him.

It is only now that Olga remembers Vershinin's wife, neglected in the arrangements; she should be billeted with her children in the drawing room but perhaps separately from her husband. We need to remember the gist of this geography.

On the face of it, it is hard to understand Chebutykin's bad timing. But watching what now happens to Anfisa, we might get an inkling: perhaps Chekhov, aware of the quirks of human nature, is hinting that it is in the nature of old people, as of children, to panic and add one crisis to another. At this inopportune moment, the exhausted old servant is suddenly gripped with terror that she will be dismissed from service:

> Olya, dearest – please don't send me away! Don't send me away!

That's out of the question, Olga, startled, assures her. What has given her such an idea?

> ANFISA: I'm getting feeble, and they'll tell me to go. 'Clear off!' they'll say. But where can I go? Where?

It is an ominous hint: who can this repeated 'they' be? What has been going on beneath stairs? As if on cue, Natasha appears.

She is here because someone has suggested setting up a fund to help the victims of the fire; she thinks it 'a splendid idea' and states baldly:

> We've got to do what we can for the poor, the rich have an obligation.

Leaving aside the question of whether the family really is rich, especially now that Natasha is draining some of their resources, this is the sort of self-satisfied cliché a sincere person might have left unsaid. And as far as getting something done is concerned, Olga is already hard at work. And the human detail we have gathered from Olga about the victims – Fedotik, the 'Kolotilin girls' – is somehow clouded over by Natasha's smug generalisations about the nameless poor. In any case everything is fine in her encapsulated world:

> Bobik and little Sophie are tucked away in bed, fast asleep, as if nothing's happened.

So there is now a new child, Sophie (a slightly affected French version of the Russian name Sofya) and we have another chance to measure the passage of time from Natasha's successive births. And it will soon emerge that Irina is twenty-four, whereas she was twenty at the start of the play, so that establishes its outer limits. At the moment Natasha has one main worry – that both children could be vulnerable to something less immediate than the fire:

> There's a 'flu epidemic in the town, I'm frightened in case the children catch it . . .

– from all those deserving poor, presumably.

Standing next to the exhausted, industrious Olga, Natasha also finds a moment to check her appearance in the mirror –

> I must look a mess . . . They tell me I've put on weight . . . it's not true.

– though with two children it would be unlikely that she hadn't.

These uncomfortable moments prepare us for one of the nastiest moments in all Chekhov's plays. At Olga's invitation, Anfisa is sitting resting, as some servants in old Russian households, almost members of the family, were accustomed to do. Pausing to note how tired Masha must (for some reason) be, Natasha comes upon the hard-working old lady, nurse to her own children, and flies at her:

> How dare you sit down in my presence! Stand up! Get out of here!
> *Anfisa exits. A pause.*
> I really can't imagine why you keep that old creature on.

Natasha's earlier gaucheries – her use of French, her cooing over the children – inspired ridicule rather than dislike; but it is becoming very hard to be tolerant of a woman who does so little to help in an emergency, and is so vicious to a faithful old servant.

And what of our put-upon heroines, whose plight we have been encouraged to feel from start to finish: do they stand up

for themselves and their dependants, or, like Andrei con-
fronted by his wife, do they put their heads in the sand? As
Anfisa now scuttles away, all that Olga, sustained by a drink of
water, will eventually manage by way of protest is that it
makes her 'depressed . . . faint . . . ill . . . drained . . . upset'
when people are treated in such a way. She is hardly more up
to the fight than Anfisa herself, and were it not for her efforts
over the fire, you might wonder who is the more useless. As for
the other sister, Masha, she remains silent; and in a moment,
rather than arguing with Natasha, she will take up her pillow
and march out of the room.

Natasha's onslaught has continued in Anfisa's absence:

> She's a peasant, she ought to be living in the country . . .
> She's completely spoilt. I must have order in the home!
> There's no room for hangers-on.

However, seeing how the land lies, she is mixing in a little
unconvincing tenderness towards her sister-in-law. Stroking
her cheek, she insists that she will be afraid of her when she
becomes her school's headmistress – an appointment which is
to be confirmed, it seems, regardless of the fact that Olga
doesn't want it. No, Natasha happens to know (through her
contact with Protopopov?) that it has all been decided: she
makes it sound more like a threat than good news.

At last Olga musters her mild protest:

> You know, you were so rude to Nanny just now . . . I'm
> sorry but I just can't bear it . . . perhaps it's just our strange
> upbringing, but I really can't abide that.

Natasha immediately apologises – not for hurting Anfisa but
for upsetting Olga: there is little reason to think that she will
ever respect Anfisa's rights. The choice of the word 'upbringing' is a good one – there really is a huge gulf between the old
world of the Prozorovs and that of Natasha. Into their leisurely
life she is bringing a ruthless practicality: everybody must earn
their keep; deaf old men can be made to wait; servants will be
punished for leaving lights on; and resting nannies are not
tolerated. It is logical and heartless, while the Prozorovs'

world is sensitive, cultivated, and increasingly unreal. And of course new despots such as Natasha can only flourish if the old guard allows them in. It is part of a transition in Russian society that Chekhov hints at in all his major plays.

The argument continues to smoulder – it is all very well for Olga to say that Anfisa has been with the family for thirty years, but as far as Natasha is concerned:

> she can't work any longer. Look, either I don't understand you, or you simply don't want to understand me. She's not fit for work, she does nothing but sit around and sleep.

Olga finally manages:

> Well, let her sit!

The director and actress have to agree how strong this is – a real confrontation or a tired demurral. Whichever, it provokes Natasha to an astonishing degree: criticised, she becomes extremely hostile. She already employs (or Andrei does) a largish staff – 'a nanny, a wet-nurse . . . a maid, a cook'; Anfisa is surely surplus to requirements, and she even becomes tearful at Olga's unfairness.

There is enough of a pause for the fire alarm to be heard again outside. Olga has had enough:

> I think I've aged ten years tonight.

However, getting no response seems to upset Natasha more than getting a contrary one. She gathers herself one last time. Aiming low, she implies that she particularly understands about the servants because she is closer to them than the pampered Olga. By now she seems to be dispossessing her sister-in-law altogether:

> You're out at school, and I'm at home – you have your schoolwork, and I have this house to run.

It is as if it weren't Olga's house as well, as if she had done nothing to help in the fire.

It gets worse and worse. Natasha stamps her foot and loses her temper: she will be mistress in her own house, and the 'thieving old hag . . . the old witch' must be out of it by tomorrow, which is just dawning. And Olga should move out of her own bedroom, as Irina did, and sleep downstairs – otherwise they are 'going to be quarrelling all the time': it doesn't occur to Natasha that she might herself be able to lessen this quarrelling. There is a first hint here of the near-psychopathic violence with which she will protect her own interests for the rest of the play.

*

Much of Chekhov's own advice on the acting of *Three Sisters* is concentrated on Act Three, and as always we ignore him at our peril. He warned that above all it should be played quietly, with the feeling that everyone is tired and wants to go to bed; no 'hullabaloo' or melodrama. Presumably this is why he plants such an important clue close to the opening:

> OLGA: This is terrible, terrible. And so exhausting . . .

Although several destinies are to be dramatically played out – an illicit love affair, a family showdown, an acceptance of marriage – the details need to emerge with maximum clarity, without false or excessive emotion, always in the context of an exceptional night slowed down by overpowering fatigue.

As part of this restraint, Chekhov also wanted all external sounds to be kept strictly under control, and insisted that he had marked down exact instructions which should not be augmented. He wrote to Olga Knipper:

> What's all the noise about? The points at which the bells are to be rung offstage are shown.

Meanwhile the shocking sequence of Natasha driving out Anfisa accentuates the crucial question of how Natasha should be played. The simplest thing to say is that she is tasteless, vulgar and domineering; a cuckoo in the Prozorovs' nest who by now seems to control their lives. But it is still vital for the actress to let us see her own point of view. In acting, you always have to make a case for the devil, playing such a character as if you were the lawyer for her defence. In fact, just as

Natasha's concern for her baby on the night of the party was real enough, her attitude now to staff sitting around unproductively might be understandable if it didn't come out in quite such a nasty way. And as far as the fire goes, she may not be helping much, but Masha and Andrei aren't either.

*

As in the previous two acts, the stage fills up by degrees. Kulygin's major preoccupation is not so much the fire as keeping tabs on his wife:

Where's Masha? It's time we went home.

He often harps on about going 'home'. Chekhov felt keenly for the financial plight of provincial schoolteachers, so we can only imagine what Kulygin's lodgings might be like; and it must be irksome for him to sense that Masha feels more at home here. Despite his general affability, his need to get her away from her sisters and brother is quite intense.

As he parks himself, at least he gives us information: the fire is finally dying down because – one blessing – the wind didn't carry it through the whole town. Not much comfort to those already made homeless, but Kulygin stretches and sits as if he had himself completed some great work:

Oh, I'm so tired.

Then he says something quite unexpected. It is either a piece of casual gallantry or a revelation:

Dearest Olga . . . You know, I often think if it hadn't been for Masha, I should have married you.

This might not seem quite the moment for such a wayward thought – or quite such a self-satisfied one: would Olga have had any say in the matter? But the idea is credible: both are schoolteachers, Olga dislikes being a spinster ('I would have loved my husband'), and they might not have made such a bad match, especially now that we are learning more of how things stand between Kulygin and Masha. And the adjective Kulygin specially finds for Olga, 'kind', is not the most obvious to apply to his actual wife.

He also confirms Olga's report on Doctor Chebutykin. He is indeed out of control; worse, he is approaching the bedroom. Kulygin's attitude to this is, like Olga's to Natasha, ineffective, but unlike hers, oddly indifferent:

> (*Laughs.*) The old rogue . . . I'm going to hide from him . . . (*Goes over to the cupboard and stands in the corner.*)

Natasha and Olga likewise take evasive action, going to 'the far end of the room'. So everyone is scurrying away from the alarming drunk, hiding in inadequate places, while the bedroom feels more and more like a thoroughfare.

After such a build-up, what we see of Chebutykin when he arrives is carefully specified by Chekhov:

> CHEBUTYKIN *enters, and crosses the room without staggering, as if he were sober.*

We are obviously supposed to pay attention to what he is about to say rather than being struck by how out of control he is. This is a particular kind of drinker, who can walk steadily in a straight line, and then speak with terrible candour. Even better, Chekhov reminds us of Chebutykin's profession by making him do an habitual thing: he looks around for a washbasin and washes his hands as if he had just completed an operation. So far he has done nothing to justify expectation. Then he speaks like a medical man, albeit one threatened by age and declining competence:

> They think because I'm a doctor I can cure all their ailments, but I know absolutely nothing, I've forgotten all I ever knew . . .

This is typical of him, self-hatred turning into hatred of others: 'To hell with them!' As for his memory, there may be little to remember anyway: in the first act he said he hadn't read anything since university, and with Andrei he avoided an awkward question by saying he'd forgotten all the answers. Worse is to come:

> Last Wednesday I was attending a woman in Zasyp Street – she died, and it was my fault she died.

Chekhov's satire on his own profession continues: Dr Astrov in *Uncle Vanya* feels responsible for killing a patient, and he also likes a drink, though not so destructively as Chebutykin.

In retrospect, this doctor's attention to his hands was like washing blood from them. It is not surprising he has hit the bottle (after, according to Olga, a two-year abstinence), though this is a terrible moment to choose. His guilt over his patient – it is only a few days ago, and we have not seen him since – gives us a reverse image of the Chebutykin we knew: shame and inadequacy have quite taken the place of bonhomie and cuddliness. He begins to wonder, with the perverse logic of the drunkard, whether he even exists, or is:

> just pretending I've got arms and legs . . . and a head.

Typically, his theme is illusion, and its connection with amnesia: if he can remember nothing of what life has taught him, perhaps his very life has been a dream.

The speech he is making appears to be a soliloquy, since he hasn't seen or doesn't acknowledge the others (hiding) on stage. But it is not the familiar Shakespearian model, when a character comes to the audience and ignores the theatre's 'fourth wall' to speak directly to them. It is more that Chebutykin is muttering to himself and we are eavesdropping on his thoughts. Some directors may disagree with this, pointing to the fact that Chebutykin is intent on giving us information – the death of the woman in Zasyp Street – which he hardly needs to repeat to himself. But this after all is a meandering conversation, in which he goes over and over things he knows quite well. In any case, unlike a Shakespearian soliloquiser, he is not quite alone: Chekhov has taken the precaution of keeping Kulygin onstage in his ineffective hideout, where we at least can see him, and accept him, in a minor way, as a participant in the scene. Also Natasha and Olga, who really are hiding, slip away in full view as he gets going, so there is a certain amount of traffic while Chebutykin speaks. By this stage in his career, Chekhov is more or less doing away with soloists.

Chebutykin tilts into tearfulness:

> Oh, if only I didn't exist!

– but as he recovers, his disgust deepens, and not only with himself. He sees that the habitual hypocrisy of the others at 'the club', talking their pretentious talk about Voltaire and Shakespeare, is just as great as his own when he pretends to be familiar with such writers. But there is no relief in this thought: even if he manages to blot out the image of all those phoneys, it is inevitably replaced by the awfulness of his patient's dead body. One vision is no better than the other – the degrading falsity of social life, and the mortal guilt of a botched treatment.

Irina, Vershinin and Tuzenbakh arrive together, in search of a little privacy in this house of refugees. The drawing room is full of people; and Irina, referring to Soliony as one of them, rather unfairly calls him 'your Soliony' to Tuzenbakh. Tuzenbakh himself is incongruously wearing a new civilian suit, and we remember that he announced in Act Two that he was quitting the service for civilian life. Vershinin 'rubs his hands in satisfaction': where Kulygin attributed the limited fire damage to the mildness of the wind, he feels that it is greatly to the credit of his soldiers:

> Well, if it hadn't been for the military, the whole town would've gone up in flames. They did splendidly!

Kulygin now steps out of his hiding place, to their surprise no doubt: there is no knowing whom one may meet in the sisters' bedroom at the moment. Chebutykin meanwhile can hardly be ignored, standing there morosely. Kulygin's attitude to the old man again lacks the due concern that Olga and now Irina show towards him:

> IRINA: You ought to go to bed, Doctor . . .
> KULYGIN (*slaps him on the back*): Bravo! *In vino veritas*, as the Romans used to say.

It is of course all very well for Kulygin: he has his own home to escape to.

Tuzenbakh now brings up a practical point. Like Natasha, he has heard talk of a relief effort for the victims of the fire; but his approach is much more helpful than hers. In fact he has been asked to organise a concert, presumably so that money can be raised for their benefit in ticket sales. It turns out that he knows that Masha is a gifted pianist, though, as Irina significantly points out, she hasn't played for some years. Tuzenbakh keeps insisting on her talent, all the more so since her husband's attitude to it turns out to be only proprietorial:

> TUZENBAKH: There's absolutely nobody in this town who appreciates music, not a soul. However, I do, and I tell you this – Masha is a superb pianist, practically a genius.
> KULYGIN: You're quite right, Baron. And I love Masha so much. She's a wonderful woman.

You can sense the two men locking horns a little on this – the insecure Kulygin at sea in these artistic matters, but somehow feeling that Masha's talent reflects well on him, while Tuzenbakh implicitly insists on her independence. Tuzenbakh keeps rubbing in the fact in that no one appreciates such things hereabouts. This issue of who in the town is genuinely cultured has arisen before: Masha believed it was only the military, implying that such local people as Kulygin and Natasha weren't. It is interesting to see Tuzenbakh, normally so obliging, taking quite a stand over this and not letting the matter rest:

> To be able to play so gloriously, and to know at the same time, that nobody, absolutely nobody appreciates it!

Kulygin would have to be stupid not to take this 'nobody, absolutely nobody' personally. He fretfully comes to what was always going to be his main point, the seemliness of public performance by a married woman:

> Yes, indeed . . . But would it be proper for Masha to take part in a concert?

There is a pause: it suggests a depth of embarrassment at such small-mindedness, as if playing the piano somehow made Masha a bohemian or worse. Kulygin then digs himself a deeper hole by admitting that his chief fear is that his headmaster, on whom he feels so dependent, might disapprove – 'he does have certain views'. Perhaps he should himself take the precaution of having a preparatory word with him.

The company remains silenced, as appalled perhaps as the audience by the teacher's cravenness; everyone can sense that behind Kulygin stands a bigoted legion of nonentities whose permission must be sought for the most natural activities. If characters such as Kulygin and Natasha occasionally arouse our sympathy, this is clearly not one of those moments: all the same, the actor needs to play the schoolteacher as genuinely afraid, a slave to society and truly uncertain what to do.

Tuzenbakh in particular, having pursued the point, suddenly says nothing. Two diversions fill the gap: Chebutykin picks up a clock and examines it, while Vershinin pointedly changes the subject, though hardly for the better. His news is that this group may soon be broken up:

> . . . they're thinking of transferring our brigade to some outpost or other. Poland they're saying, or possibly Siberia.

This of course will affect everything: the Prozorovs will be alone again without their cultured visitors, and Masha in particular without Vershinin. (As Tuzenbakh has resigned his commission, Irina, for better or worse, will not be losing him.) The news has an effect on Chebutykin too – though at his age, which must be near retirement, it is not clear whether he would expect to be going as well. But he does an extraordinary thing: whether by accident or wilfully, he:

> *drops the clock, which smashes on the floor.*

To this, Kulygin takes his usual jocularly professional tone by awarding the doctor 'C-minus for conduct' – the only language he knows for dealing with difficult situations. But it is a bad moment for everyone, and we realise how bad from Irina's blunter comment:

> That was our mother's clock.

The question of course is whether it was an accident. This will probably be ambiguous in performance, since the audience will be unlikely to be looking at the doctor at the moment it happens. So it is difficult to read the old man. Has something just upset him so much that he has become destructive, or has his unsteady physical state made him butter-fingered? Covering up, he continues his game of paradoxes: just as he wondered whether he really existed at all, he now questions whether he broke the clock:

> maybe it just looks as if I did. Maybe we don't even exist, and only imagine we do.

This is irritating of course; but it is followed by worse. Preparing to leave, he suddenly drops all his evasions:

> What are you staring at? Natasha's having an affair with Protopopov, and you can't see it . . . You're all sitting here, seeing nothing, and Natasha's having an affair with Protopopov . . .

From what we have heard – particularly the 'little drive' they took in the troika – this carries an absolute smack of truth. Chebutykin tops it off with a suggestive snatch from operetta as he leaves the room:

> (*Sings.*) 'Oh lady, please accept this fruit . . . '

So the breaking of the clock may not be the only damage done. But Chebutykin, the self-appointed truth-teller, might consider his revelation a cleansing act. Perhaps, in his own eyes, he has taken revenge on all his enemies – his pals at the club and the hypocrites here at home – with his honesty and the blunt vulgarity of his song.

A decision needs to be taken. Which of the current group – Tuzenbakh, Irina, Kulygin, Vershinin – believes Chebutykin or even knows him to be right, and is there anyone to whom it is news, shocking or otherwise? Certainly nobody comments; nobody protests that it is a preposterous idea. The impression overall is that quite a lot is kept dark in this household, and some things not spoken of at all when the company is mixed.

Vershinin steps into the breach again, filling the ambiguous silence with a remark that either means a little or a lot:

> Yes . . . (*Laughs.*) It's a strange world we live in.
> *A pause.*

He finds it easy to open up a new subject, and all the better if
it is his troubled family: he begins to describe what has
happened to them all. When the fire broke out he rushed
home from wherever he was to find that, though the house was
safe, his two little girls were standing in the doorway in their
nightgowns, their mother nowhere to be seen. They were
terrified of course, two pathetic faces in the midst of the confusion, the dogs barking and the horses bolting. He snatched
them up heroically and ran to the Prozorovs, all the time
speculating that this distress was only a small hint of the
suffering they would have to endure in their future lives – not
only in the normal course of events but because of their
inadequate mother. And sure enough (after a pause, during
which the fire alarm again rings outside), we hear that she is
in this house, 'shouting and screaming'; though quite what
about he doesn't say. His whole story, in fact, is unprovable.

At this point Masha, a preferable woman from his point of
view, arrives, perhaps having heard he was here, perhaps having got over her sulk over Natasha, and in any case still clutching the pillow she marched out with. It gives Vershinin the
chance to tell his story again for her benefit, dramatising it a
little more, turning it into something almost philosophical. The
imagery he enriches it with is of something infernal:

> . . . the whole street was glowing red with fire, there was a
> hellish uproar . . .

while his girls stood in the doorway in a lurid red light. In fact,
it seemed to him like some terrible wartime raid from 'many
years ago' when the enemy would storm a village and slaugh-
ter its inhabitants. Before Masha arrived, he seemed to be
about to draw some abstract conclusions about his daughters'
future; now, as he reaches much the same point, they are left
out of the picture:

> And given a little more time, say, two or three hundred
> years, people will look back on us with the same horror and
> scorn, our present-day life will seem hard and awkward . . .
> Oh yes, what a life that's going to be!

Having moved rapidly from the recent past through the present, he is excited by his latest vision of the future, his family

forgotten now that Masha is before him, attentive and clutching her pillow:

> (*Laughs.*) I'm sorry, I'm getting carried away again. But don't stop me please – I desperately want to talk, it's the kind of mood I'm in . . .

In fact he has already been talking for quite some time, and at an unseasonable hour. Though Tuzenbakh, Irina and Kulygin still form part of his audience, he notices that they are dropping off:

> It looks as if everyone's asleep

– so he can become more intimate:

> . . . life will be wonderful! We can only imagine what it'll be like . . .

Then he flatters Masha's family just as he did in the first act, when it made her take off her hat and stay to lunch:

> I mean, there's only the three of you in this town now, but in future generations there'll be more . . . the time's coming when everything will change, people will live as you'd like them to, you'll grow old eventually, and there'll be other people born, even better than you . . .

Considering how he started out, Vershinin's mood is amazingly transformed:

> (*Laughs.*) Oh yes, I'm in a really good mood today. I have the most damnable desire to live! . . .

– whereupon he starts to sing, a snatch from Tchaikovsky's opera *Eugene Onegin*; a well-known aria that declares that love is as possible for an old soldier as for a young man. It is obviously appropriate, and Masha shows she knows it by joining in. The two of them begin to establish a coded language, a first step into their private world:

> MASHA: Tram-tam-tam . . .
> VERSHININ: Tam-tam . . .

MASHA: Tra-ra-ra?
VERSHININ: Tra-ta-ta (*Laughs.*)

Chebutykin has just broadcast one extra-marital secret in the house; there could soon be a second.

As often when Chekhov has allowed a monologue or duologue to run undisturbed, there is a sudden surprise: young Fedotik arrives dancing and laughing, celebrating the fact that:

It's all gone! All gone! Burnt to the ground!

He is reacting with hysterical joy to the fact that he has lost all his belongings:

Not a thing left. My guitar, my camera, all my letters, all gone . . . I was going to give you a little notebook, that's burnt too.

This wonderfully eccentric moment, a buoyant response to catastrophe that the sisters could hardly manage, sounds like an overexcited version of the stoicism with which Ferapont accepted he would never go to Moscow. But of course, it's not quite as it seems: Fedotik's mood could change to tears in a moment. Cunningly Chekhov doesn't allow that to happen, as he is immediately followed on by the sinister Soliony.

Irina naturally wants to see the back of him, remembering their unpleasant exchange at the end of Act Two, but unfortunately he has seen that a rival is in this bedroom while he is excluded:

So why can the Baron come in, and I can't? . . . No, it's positively peculiar – the Baron's allowed in here, and I'm not.

As usual the effect is partly comic, especially as Soliony then sprinkles his hands with scent, which Irina later complains has 'smoked the place out'. However, given his competitive feelings for Irina, it is also an ominous moment for her lover Tuzenbakh.

Vershinin rescues this situation too, using his authority as senior officer to take Soliony out. Soliony, acceding, tries to unsettle them all with another quotation, from a Krylov fable about some high-born geese who refused to be slaughtered:

> 'The moral I might make more clear, but that would vex the geese, I fear . . . '

It is, as usual, vaguely insulting, but you can' t tell quite why. Ushering him away, Vershinin is careful to leave behind the information as to where they are going, to the ballroom: this may be for Masha's benefit, and in fact he has also found time to return to their wordless musical dialogue. This time it takes the form of a question from him:

VERSHININ: Tram–tam–tam?

– answered affirmatively by her:

MASHA: Tram–tam.

So he knows that she is co-operating; and she knows where he will be.

The hour being so late, Tuzenbakh, lulled this time by Vershinin's philosophising rather than stimulated to join in, is certainly asleep. Irina and Kulygin may be as well, as Vershinin assumed, in which case Masha's and his scene is completely private. Alternatively, the director may prefer them to be only dozing, in which case Vershinin has the job of com- municating with Masha without arousing anyone's suspicions, especially those of Kulygin, who particularly wouldn't like the singing. Tuzenbakh, though, oblivious even to Soliony's inter- ruption and Fedotik's crazy dance, is far enough gone to need waking now by his Irina. He immediately starts talking as if he had never stopped, like a tap being turned on: the man in smart civilian clothes returns to his theme of working in a brick factory, to an audience that already knows his views:

> No, I'm not talking in my sleep, I'll be starting work soon, in a brick-works, it's all arranged.

His earnest ambition is all mixed up with lyrical pleasure at seeing Irina's face at the moment of waking:

You're so pale and lovely, quite enchanting . . . it's as if
your face lights up the night air, like a moonbeam . . . Oh,
come with me Irina, we'll go away and work together! . . .

It is not really the moment for such rhapsody. We don't find
out what Irina thinks of it, as she is silent, leaving Masha to
bundle him out:

Baron, please leave.

But it is as if he wants to make up for lost talking time. On and
on he goes, recalling the scene we witnessed in Act One:

. . . it all comes back to me, a long time ago on your name-
day, how bright and cheerful you were then . . .

Sadly, he knows that something has been lost, and that their
dreams are already damaged by the passage of time:

There are tears in your eyes . . . Oh, if only I could give my
life for you, Irina!
MASHA: Baron, please go. For heaven's sake!
TUZENBAKH: I'm going, I'm going . . . (*He exits.*)

Likewise, it is hardly the moment for Kulygin to reiterate his
great love for his wife, but something seems to have got into
both men as they awake. In fact it is quite comic:

Darling Masha, my dear, sweet Masha . . .

It is important to Masha that he goes home; she prefers to stay
near to her sisters, and to Vershinin. The women's main task
after the fire now seems to be clearing the room of garrulous
men; but one has to admire Kulygin's tenacity, his ability to
turn the most direct insult – Masha's use of his beloved Latin
– into a form of happiness:

KULYGIN: My wife's so good and kind . . . I love you, my
one and only . . .
MASHA (*irritated*): *Amo, amas, amat, amamus, amatis,
amant* . . .
KULYGIN (*laughs*): Really, an amazing woman! Yes, we got
married seven years ago, and it seems like only yesterday . . .

And I'm so very, very happy!

MASHA: And I'm so very, very bored!

Within a few minutes of doing so with Olga, he is calling
another woman 'kind': one thing Masha really isn't, to him at
least. He dwells on the word as if to will it into existence, this
genial but unlikeable pedant: true kindness is absent from his
life. At this moment, however, Masha has other things on her
mind than sentimental men, or even interesting ones like
Vershinin. There is, in fact, a real problem in the family, a big
fact simply not being discussed, and it was ticking away inside
her when she walked out on Natasha:

> . . . I can't keep silent. I'm talking about Andrei . . . he's
> mortgaged this house to the bank, and his wife's pocketed
> the money. I mean, this house isn't just his, it belongs to all
> four of us! He surely knows that, if he's got any decency.

So Andrei, father of two children, besieged by debts from his
gambling and perhaps from his wife's tendency to live beyond
their means, has borrowed more money from the bank. He has
used the house as security and hasn't consulted those with a
moral and probably legal right to know. It is obviously very
serious, but Kulygin, again faced with somebody else's problem, minimises it:

> Masha, why bring this up now? What does it matter?
> Andrei owes everybody money . . .

Well of course it matters a great deal, but not to him. Intol-
erant of her other ties, he would prefer to isolate himself and
Masha in his ivory tower:

> It's not as if we're poor. I have my work, I teach at the school,
> and I give private lessons . . . I'm an honest, simple man . . .
> *Omnia mea mecum porto*, as they say.

Perhaps he feels his manhood as a husband has been threatened: she is worrying about a house she no longer lives in, as if
she wasn't really committed to him. Worse, she wants him out
of it:

> Fyodor, go home, please.

But, as we are learning, there can be an iron will behind Kulygin's accommodations: yes, he will considerately leave her alone for a little while, but he will be near at hand, hardly out of sight:

> Have a little rest for a half-hour or so, and I'll wait downstairs. Try and sleep . . . (*Exits.*) I'm so very, very happy . . .

This is not what Masha was hoping for.

Irina, more or less silent since Chebutykin dropped the clock, has been roused by Masha's complaint about their brother. Now the subject has been broached, her own floodgates open. She is as wretched about Andrei's decline as Masha, but her response – a character difference between them – has more sorrow in it than blame. At the moments when she comes close to passing judgment, she tends to break down into tears. She sees that Natasha has made Andrei 'mean-minded' and 'old', his early ambitions having been so abandoned that only yesterday he was boasting of being a member of the district council presided over by Protopopov. It is very much implied that his appointment is a squalid consolation thrown out by Protopopov in return for giving up his rights to his wife:

> The whole town's talking about it, laughing behind his back . . .

So Chebutykin's bombshell was largely a matter of exposing what everybody knew already. Worse, Andrei is the only one who doesn't know – so it can't even be discussed among them privately.

Even the sound of Andrei's violin has turned sour; once it thrilled them as a measure of talent and optimism, but now it accompanies a shameful refusal to engage with the world:

> When everybody rushes out to help with the fire, he sits in his room, not the least bit concerned. Playing his fiddle. (*Agitated.*) It's terrible, terrible! (*Begins to cry.*) I can't stand it, I can't take any more of this . . .

It is unclear whether it would be in Masha's nature to comfort her sister in her extremity: fortunately Olga comes back in time to take the full impact. Andrei was simply the trigger: Irina intuitively sees his failure as a symptom of their family's greater collapse, particularly that of her own life. She can no longer avoid the point, and grief pours out of her:

> Where has it all gone? Where? Where is it? Oh God in heaven! I've forgotten everything, everything . . . It's all gone right out of my head . . .

Chekhov's genius is to make this distress, intensifying so alarmingly, almost comically specific:

> I can't remember the Italian for 'window' or 'ceiling' . . .

Such a complaint about forgetting things makes her sound oddly like Chebutykin, whose position is in every other way so different. But she also has the young person's paradoxical terror that there isn't much time left:

> life's passing me by, and it'll never return.

Clearly Tuzenbakh hasn't succeeded in diverting her from her pipe-dream with the alternative of useful work:

> we'll never get to Moscow, we'll never leave here . . .

The audience will feel sorry for her at this point: they may also want to give her a shake for not being more practical. But it is as if she can hear that criticism coming, and answers it: she has made a real effort, she insists. She has taken a demoralising job in the telegraph office, then joined the town council as her brother did the district council: all this has done for her at the great age of twenty-four is to dry up her brain and make her 'thin, and old, and ugly' (at least in her own eyes):

> . . . there's no satisfaction in it, absolutely none, and time's passing, and I feel as if I'm moving further and further away from a genuine, beautiful life, and heading into some kind of abyss.

Much as Olga tries –

> Don't cry, darling, don't cry . . . It hurts me . . .

– there is no comfort at hand for such a mixture of panic and sorrow, of exaggeration and clear-sightedness. The only thing is to let it subside in its own time:

> I won't, I won't cry . . . Enough . . . Look, I've stopped crying . . . It's over . . .

Olga has sensed that she must wait for this moment before her calm voice can be heard. The world is not perfect, and the answer is clear to her, however disappointing to Irina:

> I'm speaking to you now as a sister, as a friend . . . If you want my advice, you should marry the Baron . . .

Look at the advantages – Tuzenbakh's obvious decency and kindness, his respectability. Words that might be bitter in another mouth become, in Olga's hard-won philosophy, toughly persuasive, and, preferably, played without personal bitterness:

> I mean, women don't marry for love, they do it out of duty. At least, that's what I think, and I'd marry without love. I'd marry anyone who asked me, as long as he was a decent person. I'd even marry an old man . . .

Although this must be light-years from Irina's romantic ideals, interestingly she does not reject it. Nor does she accept it; her reaction is to keep talking, around the subject, as people will when they are privately considering an idea:

> I kept waiting, waiting for us to move to Moscow, and I'd meet my true love there. I've dreamt about him, loved him . . . But it turned out to be nonsense, all of it . . .

Her tone is no longer hysterical or desperate. The girl who sat up in bed drinking coffee and dreaming, for whom the busy metropolis, was, for all its problems, a place where men rode on white chargers, seems to have grasped the reality. If she has grown up, more's the pity but still more the necessity. Olga knows that for Irina to admit even this much is a victory – she hugs her sister and even chances a little humour:

> When the Baron left the service, and came to see us in his civilian clothes, he looked so awful that I actually started to

cry . . . And he asked me, 'Why are you crying?' What could I tell him?

Her point is that that doesn't matter: if they were to marry it would be 'quite different', and she would welcome him into the family with open arms.

Perhaps Irina laughs at the memory of the Baron in his inappropriate suit; perhaps she is reassured by Olga's loyalty. In fact humour is about to be the key to recovery all round. Natasha happens to cross the stage:

> . . . *from right to left in silence, holding a candle.*
> MASHA (*sits up*): The way she's going around, you'd think it was her that started the fire.

This should get a laugh. For the sisters, mockery may be their only way of enduring Natasha: it binds them together and gives them the illusion of strength. Olga's mock-shocked reaction to this outspokenness is hard to take seriously:

> And you're silly, Masha. You're the silliest person in this family.

Silly is hardly the word to use, and indeed she can't keep her protest up:

> If you'll forgive my saying.

This moment can be played in a number of ways; but in view of what Masha is about to admit, it is attractive to feel that the sisters are close in spite of everything.

If so, it doesn't last. Masha has a secret, a desperate one, and this is the moment she chooses to unburden herself, a third confessor (after Chebutykin and Irina) in this extraordinary night. Perhaps it is in her character wilfully to break the mood in the room; perhaps she has been encouraged by that moment of harmony and expects what she says to go well:

> I've a confession to make, my dear sisters . . . It's my secret, but you ought to know . . .

She has now to call a spade a spade – a thing this family has difficulty with, certainly when it comes to a sexual scandal – and she does it almost voluptuously:

> I'm in love . . . I'm in love with that man . . . Oh, why not come out with it? I'm in love with Vershinin . . .

No wonder Olga disappears behind her screen, her ears covered, trying to escape such obscene repetitions. She pretends, improbably, that she can ignore them as if she were deaf:

> (*Goes behind her screen.*) That's enough, I'm not listening to you anyway!

But Masha is experiencing the rapture of confession, of surrendering herself to the truth:

> . . . eventually I fell in love with him . . . I fell in love with his voice, the things he said, his unhappy life, his two little girls . . .

To Olga, Masha was 'silly' a moment ago; now her disembodied voice calls her 'stupid', while simultaneously declaring:

> I don't care, I can't hear you.

Certainly it is the last news on earth Olga and Irina want to hear – terrible enough tonight and a source of misery in the future – and perhaps as immoral in their eyes as Protopopov's adulterous dealings with Natasha. Since Olga will have nothing to do with it – Masha dismisses her as 'stupid' herself – it is Irina who has to listen silently to her wayward sister telling her what falling in love is all about. This is moments after recovering from her own breakdown and being advised to marry even without love. In some way Masha is aware of this paradox: she sees that what she feels can hardly lead to happiness, while for Irina happiness might lie in forgetting about love altogether. But she includes Irina in the general muddle:

> Oh my dear Irina, how are we going to survive? What's to become of us? . . .

She warns her that to 'read a love story' – or presumably to dream of romance – in no way prepares you for the awesome reality, which can isolate you from the rest of the world rather than putting you in step with it. It is, for her, a moment when:

> it's obvious that nobody knows anything, we each have to work it out on our own.

Any sensual pleasure she took in her announcement has quickly died. Irina is silent (the actress can decide what she is thinking) and Olga has gone. Bleakly, Masha has to draw a veil over what might happen next, risk losing her sisters' approval entirely, perhaps never confide in them again:

> I've confessed to you, now I'll keep silent . . .

*

As for this great middle movement of the act, we should let Chekhov speak for himself again. He writes to Stanislavsky during rehearsals:

> You write that Natasha, making her rounds of the house at night in Act Three, puts out the lights and looks for burglars under the furniture. But it seems better to me for her to cross the stage in a straight line, without looking at anybody or anything, like Lady Macbeth, with a candle. It's quicker and more frightening that way.

He also continues his running commentary to Olga Knipper, playing Masha. When she and Vershinin start to sing together (it is not quite clear whether he is referring to their first two exchanges or the one that is coming shortly) he declares that Vershinin should do his 'Tram-tam-tam' as a question, and Masha hers as an answer:

> It should strike you as such an original thing to say that you utter it with a slight smile . . . You should say 'tram-tram' and give a little laugh, not a loud one, just a hint . . .

For once, he even seems a little over-attentive. The next day he turns to Masha's confession:

Darling, Masha's repentance in Act Three isn't repentance at all, it's no more than a frank talk. Act it with feeling, but not desperately. Don't shout, put in some smiles, even if only a few, and in general act it so that people feel the tiredness of the night. And make them feel you're cleverer than your sisters – or at least that you think yourself cleverer.

*

Masha finally said that in keeping her story secret she would go silently out of her mind, like the deluded hero of Gogol's *Diary of a Madman*. What answer, in any case, could Olga or Irina give her at this moment? Chekhov saves them with a surprise, as he often does when language falters: abruptly, the story returns to Andrei. He has abandoned his violin and come out into the world, so it must be important. He arrives in a fluster, with Ferapont at his heels even at this time of night, for once not his obliging confidant but simply a nuisance. For the moment, Andrei seems to have learned his manners from his wife, and in an unpleasant echo of Natasha's treatment of Anfisa, he insists that Ferapont take notice of his official status:

> In the first place, I'm not Master Andrei to you, but Your Honour!

Ferapont hears this all right, and adjusts to it without a pause, as a servant knows to. What he is asking is in any case simple – permission for the overworked firemen to take a short cut through the Prozorovs' orchard to get to the river for water. It is not difficult to understand, especially when it has been repeated, as Andrei complains, 'half a dozen times', but he has seemed quite unable to concentrate on the request:

> I can't understand you.

Once the penny drops, it is easy to agree:

> All right. Tell them it's all right.

– though, again like his wife, he seems to have developed a contempt for the working man:

Honestly, they get on my nerves.

This is a long way from the young intellectual who dreamed of scholarly fame, more the gambler and renegade, at odds with himself in every way.

He faces his sisters – or tries to. Olga obediently comes out from behind her screen, but without a word; Irina, equally silent, disappears behind hers, so he is no better off. All he claims to want is the key to a certain cupboard. His visible sisters say nothing as Olga hands him the key. Their faces either soften his mood a little or embarrass him into small talk:

What a huge fire! It's dying down now.

This is hardly news; and all Olga's hard work over the conflagration must be a silent reproach to him, who has done nothing. He becomes a little more human, realising that to be so irritable with Ferapont was to let himself down:

I came out with something stupid . . . Your Honour, indeed!

You might think this would elicit something, but the silence is still deafening:

A pause.
Why don't you say something, Olya?
A pause.

He demands, reasonably enough, to have matters out. However it is a bad start to describe the three of them as 'sulking', as if they were silly girls rather than sisters he is disinheriting. As with other things in the act, this seems hardly the time for the showdown; on the other hand, it can't be all that common for the four of them to be alone together as a family, so in a sense the moment may not be badly chosen:

ANDREI: . . . we can get to the bottom of it now, once and for all. Exactly what is it you have against me? Come on, tell me.

This demand will be as little welcome to Olga as the news about Masha. Fire, the unpleasantness with Natasha, Chebutykin's performance, Irina's distress and Masha's awful confession,

morning approaching and no sleep – enough is enough. She
also detects the self-righteousness in Andrei, his unwillingness
to admit to anything, though she does use the familiar form of
his name:

> Leave it, Andryusha. We'll talk about it tomorrow.
> (*Upset.*) What a dreadful night it's been.

But Andrei won't wait till tomorrow, and he asks again – more
mildly perhaps, but with the same unfortunate turn of phrase:

> Don't get upset. I'm asking you perfectly calmly: what have
> you got against me? Come right out with it.

However, luck is not with him. At this very moment there is a
familiar snatch of song from somewhere near the room:

> VERSHININ *is heard offstage: 'Tram-tam-tam!'*

This signal to Masha is a spark set to a fuse. She could not be
more decisive: she answers 'loudly' and stands up, Chekhov
specifies, as if to make it absolutely clear that this is the end of
her time with Andrei and her sisters:

> Tra-ta-ta!

Even her hurried advice to Andrei as she prepares to leave is
phrased to separate herself from 'them', as if their business no
longer had anything to do with her:

> Goodbye, Andrei. Just leave them, they're exhausted . . .
> you can have it out with them tomorrow (*Exits.*)

It is a pity in a way: the siblings might – just might – have got
to the bottom of their difficulties at this moment. However life
is not like that, and so an unrepeatable opportunity is lost.

Having hastily gathered herself, Masha leaves the room,
assuredly not to go home to Kulygin. Now it is too late for anything; to Olga, Masha's sudden departure is another reason
the long day should end:

> Yes, Andrei, let's put it off till tomorrow. (*She goes behind
> her screen.*)

After all the traffic through this room, we are left with an extraordinary image: a man in front of two screens, speaking to an invisible and unresponding audience – another upheaval by Chekhov of the soliloquy convention. In these unhelpful circumstances, Andrei must say his piece, and hope that, like someone in a confessional, it will be easier if he doesn't see the listener's face. But that leads to another miscalculation: he has forgotten that in an argument it may be best to start with a concession, some acknowledgment that the other side may have a point. In fact he does everything the wrong way round; and perhaps because he has rehearsed it too often, his speech lacks spontaneity. The way he orders his argument, as if under written headings, is certainly alienating. At the end of each firmly-made point he leaves a pause, but no reply is forthcoming – it is a true judgment on him, as he is not being honest enough to deserve one.

First of all, he digs in his heels: Natasha, for some inexplicable reason, has been disliked by the sisters since the day he married her, but he must insist that she is:

> a fine, honest woman, upright and honourable – that's my opinion.

The unsettling silence continues:

> I love and respect my wife, do you understand? I respect her, and I insist that other people respect her too.

It is a pitiful argument – as if respect could be compulsory:

> I'll say it again, she's a decent, honest woman

– in fact, this is so obvious a truth to him that their:

> complaints, I'm sorry to say, are nothing but sheer bloody-mindedness.

This is no better than saying they are sulking. It is a measure of Andrei's baffled panic that he could imagine such unyielding pomposity would go down well. There is another large pause.

Secondly, he supposes part of the sisters' annoyance with him is that he has failed in his aim of becoming a Professor. But the intellectual life isn't everything: he is proud to be on the executive of the district council:

> in my view that's just as exalted and sacred an office as any academic post.

This may sound ridiculous to us, but in view of the *zemstvo*'s idealistic origins it is a defensible position. The actor of Andrei should believe that he means what he says – or at least needs to convince himself that a man could do more good in this way than by sitting in a library indulging his enthusiasms.

Yet more silence, and there is no longer any evading the biggest point, which Andrei knows is very serious:

> Thirdly . . . I've something more to say . . . I mortgaged the house without asking your permission . . . Well, that was wrong of me, and I'm asking you to forgive me . . .

The reasons, as they all know, have to do with his gambling losses, though even that risky activity could be justified, he feels, because of his vulnerable position – the sisters:

> have an annuity, and I've never had anything . . . no income, I mean . . .

All the same, a thirty-five thousand rouble debt is unlikely to be reduced by spending more at the tables, and Andrei doesn't seem like a man strong enough to know when to stop.

And the time for forgiveness is gone. This was barely an apology at all, and Andrei gets no quarter. The silence continues: his inability to assess an audience he can't see is becoming comically painful. Then, as with Andrei's entrance on top of Masha's confession, Chekhov pulls off an exceptional piece of stagecraft. The extreme tension is loosened by the sudden brief appearance of Kulygin, putting his head round the door, in desperate search of his wife:

> Isn't Masha here? (*Anxiously.*) Where can she be? That's odd . . . *(Exits.)*

It is not so much odd as catastrophic for him: he has been waiting downstairs and she hasn't appeared there, but she is not here either. And he hasn't seen Vershinin recently either.

Andrei ignores him, but though he stubbornly keeps going, his grip on his argument has weakened and he is struggling. Either to himself or us, he complains:

> They're not listening. Natasha's a first-class, honest person.

Perhaps he will come to believe this if he repeats it enough. But he can't keep saying the same thing, and emotion begins to seep from him:

> When I got married, I thought we'd be so happy . . . all of us . . . But oh, my God . . . (*Begins to cry.*) Oh, my dear sisters, my good, kind sisters, don't listen to me, don't believe a word of it . . . (*Exits.*)

And in these few honest moments, our regard and sympathy for him return – no longer the bully and self-justifier, he is the young man playing his springtime violin once more. We should feel acutely how harshly life can deal with the hopeful. Like some wretched jack-in-the-box, Kulygin is back:

> Where's Masha? She's still not here? Most peculiar . . .
> (*Exits.*)

He must have been rushing helplessly all over the house, upstairs and down: the swiftness of his return shows how rapidly he's been doing it. When we saw him somewhat like this before, at the end of Act Two, Masha was harmlessly out in the street, but this is different: the awful meaning of her latest disappearance is dawning on him.

It is against this mass of upset that Irina takes calm stock. The alarm is heard again, ringing across an empty stage. She can also hear a knocking on the floor, like the one in the first act but from the drawing room this time, and Olga confirms that it is the drunken doctor, banging about.

> IRINA: What a dreadful night!

She looks out from behind her screen. Two things are uppermost in her mind: Vershinin's report that the brigade are to leave them, and Olga's realistic advice about marriage. She turns them over carefully:

> . . . oh, Olya!
> OLGA: What is it now?

She is coming to a decision in front of us, unlike any she has reached before, and her tone is older and quieter:

> Listen, my dearest . . . I respect the Baron, I think highly of him, he's a fine man, and I shall marry him . . .

Multiple disruptions have provoked calm practicality in her. The new effect is striking, but incomplete: she has not really changed so much, because there is a condition:

> Just as long as we go to Moscow! Oh please, please, let's go to Moscow! There's nowhere in the world like Moscow! We've got to go, Olya, we must!

This is the Irina we know, as alone as she was at the end of the second act with her most heartfelt wish. There is no indication that Olga comes out from behind her screen.

*

One of the vivid things about this act is its lack of ambiguity: there are really not many alternatives for director and cast to pursue in realising each moment. The characters have been so carefully built up in the first half of the play that they now seem to have their own volition; thrown into circumstances as abnormal as these, they reveal unmistakable truths. Kulygin, who has been assembled as part-buffoon, part-bully and part-victim of an unhappy marriage, started the act as pompously as ever but, unable to locate his wife, advertised his pathetic insecurity about her. Olga was, not unusually, tired, but her conscience dictated that she find strength to deal with the emergency; Natasha was nothing if not true to her overbearing self. Vershinin's and Masha's relationship moved inevitably towards its decisive point. Though Chekhov, subject to the censor, had to be more discreet about sex than a contemporary playwright might be, we can assume that by the end of this act, somewhere in the house, with dawn breaking – and his wife and children in the drawing-room – the two of them are together. It is all exceptionally clear and logical, having been so well prepared: the characters do exactly what they would do, now that the audience comes to think of it.

But there have also been surprises: the abnormality of the night caused emotional as well as practical disruption. Anfisa, usually imperturbable, was gripped by terror for her place in the house. Irina could no longer escape her overwhelming sense of premature failure and showed emotions more extreme than we thought she had. Chebutykin revealed the cost of being so carefully detached from life: a terrible sense of waste and unworthiness. Andrei, briefly attempting to dissemble to his sisters, demonstrated the same depth of self-hatred as Irina. It has been a scene full of intimate confessions, overheard not only by us but by other, often concealed, characters.

No one tonight was physically where they would expect to be, but cheek by jowl with people that they might prefer not to be with. As many as seven found themselves cramped together in Olga's and Irina's bedroom, a place most of them would never imagine entering at all. There were two beds and nowhere obvious to sit; characters comically hid in the corners of the room. It is indeed very pointed that Soliony alone was ex-cluded, since the room had become a base for everyone else.

As Chekhov insisted, everyone was exhausted, and therefore unpredictable. Even as life eventually returned to normal after the fire, individual crises kept breaking in, puncturing the steadying rhythm. When Masha confessed her love for Vershinin, a new energy was released just as everyone was ready for bed. Equally inappropriately, Andrei arrived, blustering, just as we thought the act might be closing. Into the middle of his anguish Kulygin incongruously burst in pursuit of Masha – twice. Even when everything seemed settled and at peace, Chebutykin banged on the floor and Irina decided to marry the Baron. In the end she was the only one in the right emo-tional tempo, making her great decision quietly and clear-sightedly.

The important thing, as always, has been to listen carefully to the rhythms Chekhov has provided and to observe his directions – either such literal matters as the continuous ringing of the firebell, or the precise indications to the actors at the front of their speeches. Olga was described as 'upset' rather than, say, 'harassed' to emphasise that her feelings about the night were not just a matter of the fire. In reply, Andrei was 'rather embarrassed'. It would be too simple to say that if all this is done the act will play itself, but it is likely that if we simply listen to Chekhov this may be the least difficult part of the play to realise.

Act Four

The fourth act of *Three Sisters*, like the third, starts with a surprise. More time has passed, though it is not at first clear how much. During the course of the act Tuzenbakh will say that he has loved Irina for five years, and he certainly did at the start of the action, so the overall span cannot be longer than that. At times like this, the play feels like an animated album of snapshots taken across a long period. Apart from the arrival of Bobik, the jump between Act One and Two was marked by an obvious change in Andrei; between Act Two and Three Sophie had been born; now, in Act Four, Kulygin has shaved off his moustache. Chebutykin is cheerful again, Second Lieutenants Fedotik and Rodé are in full parade uniforms, and for the first time we are in the open air.

Fedotik, who seems to have the knack of calling a spade a spade but also of remaining cheerful in the face of disaster, gives a clue as to what is happening:

> TUZENBAKH: . . . Goodbye, my dear friend!
> IRINA: *Au revoir!*
> FEDOTIK: No, not *au revoir*, it's goodbye, I'm afraid – we'll never see each other again.

So the brigade is leaving today; it cannot be so very long after Act Three, when this was predicted. It transpires, as a result of an untypical joke from Kulygin about one of the officers marrying a Polish wife, that Poland is, as Vershinin half-expected, its destination. However Chebutykin is still comfortably installed in the house because, for no evident reason, he is following a day later. The long night of the fire forgotten along with any other setbacks during the stay, the company is marking the departure with champagne and photographs on the porch. Even Kulygin, who has ample reason for wanting the soldiers gone, is paradoxically moved by the finality of it all:

> Look at this, I'm crying too!

In fact, he may weep more frequently these days.

Much as Irina may try to soften the blow:

> We'll meet again some day.

– the remorseless Fedotik will have no false comfort:

> What, in ten or fifteen years, say? We'll barely recognise
> each other by then, we'll shake hands very coldly . . .

This Russian dismay at the hugeness of a country in which friends can be easily lost without recovery is being dealt with in two different ways: hope against hope (typically enough) from Irina, and truth-telling from a minor character. Fedotik is matched in ruthlessness by Rodé, who ignores Tuzenbakh's fond hope that they will all write to each other, preferring to say a last goodbye to the unique atmospherics, the household gods you might say, of the place:

> Coo-eee! Coo-eee!
> *A pause.*
> Farewell, echo!

Some more facts are expressed, important for the audience to hear clearly: the soldiers will be gone within an hour; Soliony, alone of the unit, is travelling by river, the rest as foot soldiers. All six battery divisions in the town will be gone by tomorrow. The descending silence will be deep indeed, and we realise that, beyond the Prozorovs', all this time there were other households where the military were entertained, no doubt with their own dramas.

All that is left is to say goodbye to Masha, who is in the depths of the garden; and also for Fedotik to give one final little gift, not to Irina this time, but unexpectedly to Kulygin:

> This is for you, a keepsake . . . a notebook and a pencil.

It may be that he knows it is the schoolteacher who might be in need of comfort. Chebutykin is overlooked, and perhaps has done all he can to be so:

CHEBUTYKIN: They forgot to say goodbye to me.
IRINA: And what about you?
CHEBUTYKIN: I forgot as well.

This is nonsense talk – he could hardly have forgotten as he was sitting there watching, he just didn't trouble himself. One of his objects these days seems to be to keep a low profile. In a year's time, though, when he next comes to see the Prozorovs, retired and on his army pension, he promises to:

. . . turn over a new leaf . . . I'll be so quiet, and well . . . well-behaved, and respectable . . .

Perhaps no one has quite forgotten his disgrace in Act Three; certainly Irina, who watched him drop her mother's clock, has a firm point of view:

You really ought to turn over a new leaf, my dear. You really should try.

The doctor barely acknowledges this, but takes characteristic refuge behind a newspaper, humming a little tune:

Ta-ra-ra boom-dee-ay, ta-ra-ra boom-dee-ay . . .

This is, in its Russian version, the chorus of an American music-hall song recently arrived in Europe – the accompanying verses varied from country to country, but always had a distinctly sexual overtone. It had also been adopted as a military marching tune. So every time Chebutykin uses it in this act, it is a reminder of the soldier's life, with a certain coarseness. It is enough for Kulygin to protest at now; recovered from the recent farewells, he doubts whether turning over a new leaf would ever be an option for the old man:

You're incorrigible, Doctor. Quite incorrigible!

This brings him enough into focus for Irina and Chebutykin to make fun of his changed appearance:

IRINA: Fyodor's shaved off his moustaches. I can't look at him . . .

CHEBUTYKIN: I wish I could say what your phizzog looks like now, but I can't.

It's difficult to know why his being clean-shaven would cause such a stir, but the cause of it is typical:

It's the done thing nowadays . . . Our headmaster's shaved off his whiskers, and since I've been made deputy, I've shaved mine off too.

He will put up with anything, it seems, to be in line with his superior:

Nobody likes it, but I don't care. I'm happy. With or without whiskers, I'm a happy man.

This is a patent untruth: what he means is that whiskers are the least of his troubles.

Masha was briefly seen in the distance earlier; now Andrei takes her place at the bottom of the garden, wheeling Sophie in her pram. As he does so, a new story starts up, but it has nothing to do with him – in this way Chekhov creates the illusion of continuous, varied life behind a changing main focus. This focus is now on Irina, worried that something happened 'yesterday, on the boulevard', apparently involving Soliony and Tuzenbakh. She expects Chebutykin to know about it, but he is keeping quiet, barricaded behind his newspaper and his nonchalant attitude:

What's it matter anyway?

Tuzenbakh himself would prefer the subject dropped, just as Kulygin wants to keep it going:

TUZENBAKH: Oh, stop, that's enough. Honestly! (*Waves his hand dismissively and goes into the house.*)

But Kulygin has no such scruples about telling Irina the bad news. It seems that Soliony and Tuzenbakh met and quarrelled, Soliony picking on the Baron as usual, but this time the normally patient Tuzenbakh couldn't refrain from returning the insult. The result was as predictable as clockwork – a duel.

Kulygin also knows that one of their problems is that Soliony has fallen for Irina – a thing he is happy to talk about openly, since he can well understand the feeling: she is, after all, of the same blood as his beloved Masha. His inability to keep a secret is matched by his tendency to keep returning to the subject of himself: when Chebutykin, only slightly less of a gossip, interrupts to dismiss the whole story as 'bunkum', Kulygin can't help telling a little school story:

> I heard about a teacher in a seminary once, who wrote 'bunkum' on a student's essay, and he thought it was a Latin word! (*Laughs.*)

It is only a momentary distraction, the memory of it the briefest of pleasures. Returning to his theme, Kulygin pays tribute to Irina – 'a very pretty girl' – but is careful to praise Masha in the same breath, so that she will seem in no way inferior:

> And she's so like Masha, always deep in thought. You've a gentler nature, though, Irina. Of course, Masha has a very nice nature too. Yes, I do love Masha.

This loyalty under strain is pathetic and quite touching: Kulygin knows he has married the wrong woman. He has already said he might have preferred Olga, and now Masha's abrasively unpredictable nature is suiting him less that Irina's might have done. It is a brilliant piece of writing: in a few indirect words, with their careful repetitive rhythm, Chekhov has left us in no doubt of the speaker's deep unhappiness. Kulygin knows Vershinin is leaving today; Masha is not beside him but on her own somewhere; he surely knows of the relationship, and how she must be feeling at this moment of goodbye. His dogged determination not to criticise a wife everyone now senses to be unfaithful admits his huge defeat but also gives him a certain dignity: the actor should find it easy to keep our guarded sympathy alive.

All the normality is beginning to feel forced: something is being evaded, some story lurking, preoccupying everyone. For one thing, Irina is jumpy about all the secrecy. A cry is heard from the depths of the garden. It is only the sound that Rodé used to test the echo:

> Coo-eee! Coo-eee!

– but for the first time it sounds other than a merry greeting.
(In Russian it is '*Ay! Gop-gop!*', perhaps a stranger sound than
in English.) It significantly startles Irina:

> Everything seems to frighten me today.

As with Kulygin a moment ago, Chekhov is revealing her state
of mind in the most economical way. What, apart from further
insults between Soliony and her fiancé, is Irina nervous about?
Could it be what she now describes as her new life, which,
considering how much she and Tuzenbakh have discussed it,
she surely welcomes? She is packed and ready to leave home,
she is to be married tomorrow; the same afternoon they will
leave for the brickworks, where presumably he is to work
(whether clerically or physically is never quite clear), and the
next day she will start a life of teaching. Tuzenbakh will have
got exactly what he asked for, though we can only guess how
this sensitive and educated man, in his civilian suit, will fare at
work. Irina's new life sounds more promising: passing her
teaching exam must have given confidence to someone in such
despair of her intellect that she once couldn't remember the
Italian for 'window':

> You know, when I passed the exam to be a teacher, I
> actually cried for joy, I was so happy . . .

But now she is frightened. There is a pause, then:

> The cart'll be here soon for my things.

As to her becoming a teacher, what is Kulygin's attitude to
such an idealistic novice joining his profession? Not altogether
welcoming, but certainly perceptive:

> Well, that's as may be, but it somehow doesn't seem serious.
> A lot of ideas, yes, but not much serious thought.

We would probably have to agree with that. But today, his own
anxiety has made him good-natured:

> Still, I wish you well, from the bottom of my heart.

He is not the only one. Hearing these words, a sort of goodbye, Chebutykin unexpectedly finds his voice. The great evader is suddenly as emotional as when he was drunk, but in a much healthier way, as sorrowful as when his name-day gift was laughed at:

> My dear, darling girl . . . My sweet child . . . You're going so far away, we'll never catch you up . . . And I'm left behind, like some migrating bird that's grown too old to fly.

This moving admission is almost too much for him: it is followed by a pause in which his emotion resounds, and he immediately has to cover up. Fortunately there is a running joke close at hand:

> You know, Kulygin, you shouldn't have shaved off your moustache.

Kulygin's next line might show how offended he is; but equally he may sense that this was Chebuytkin's way of recovering his equilibrium, so the reproach could be quite mild:

> Oh, that's enough from you.

Still, the important matter of the scene is not quite being acknowledged. Tuzenbakh's and Soliony's quarrel is one thing, but there is something else, and Kulygin edges towards it:

> Yes, the soldiers are leaving today, and soon everything'll be back to normal. You know, people can say what they like, Masha's a fine, honest woman. I love her very much, and I'm thankful for the way things have turned out.

What he might have said was, 'Thank God Vershinin and his battery are leaving for ever. I stand up for Masha whatever she's done, I forgive her, I know her value; my love is intact, and I'm glad she's with me again, temptation almost removed.' But of course, this being Chekhov, he doesn't quite say that, and being Kulygin he certainly doesn't. He knows that in a matter of moments he will have to witness his wife's distress at the loss of Vershinin, and find a way of getting her through it. Or, it must have occurred to him, should he let someone else do the job, a sister for instance? In his nervousness about the next few minutes, he is proving the most verbose character on stage: his tongue keeps rattling away, insisting that his life is a happy one. Now he tries to construct a moral tale about the difference between one person's fate and another's, drawing on his comforting store of school anecdotes. He knows someone who works in the Excise Office: in fact, he was at school with him until the man, Kozyrev, was expelled for not being able to 'make head or tail' of the Latin construction of *'ut consecutivum'*. Kozyrev is ill and poor these days, and whenever they meet Kulygin always reminds him of the cause of all his problems:

> I say, 'Hello, *ut consecutivum*'. 'Yes,' he says, '*Consecutivum*, that's it exactly!' and then he starts coughing . . .

We might wonder why Kozyrev doesn't punch Kulygin. It is as if we might be developing too much sympathy for the cuckolded schoolmaster and need reminding how annoying he can be. In the same vein, ruffled as his feathers are today, he continues to preen:

> Whereas I've been lucky all my life, I'm a happy man, I've even been awarded the Order of St Stanislaus, Second Class . . . Of course, I'm a clever man, cleverer than most, but that's no guarantee of happiness . . .

Once again, this is a piece of perfect character writing, and a gift for the actor. It is what Chekhov does best: we learn all about Kulygin from what he says, but not in the way he wants us to. If he is a happy man, and not because he's clever, what is the reason? Because he is proud of his deep, stubborn resilience? He feels contempt for his old schoolfriend, satisfaction about himself, and it is all based on insecurity. We sympathise with his pain, despise his vanity, marvel at his unkindness but also at his determination.

Clearly, marriage brings no comfort, though the prospect of it may be easing Irina's load a little. The play's two adulteries are now considered side by side, as Kulygin is interrupted by music from inside the house – an old piano favourite, 'The Maiden's Prayer'. This indicates the presence of Natasha's lover,

Protopopov. To Kulygin, listening to it, it must seem that there is no moral order left in the world. No wonder he staves off all thoughts of Protopopov with:

> Hasn't our headmistress arrived yet?

The visitor from the Council is equally hateful to Irina: he is one of the reasons she looks forward to leaving home. We now learn a little more of the life she will be losing. Olga lives at the school these days (Natasha having presumably ousted her), though she is coming back today to say goodbye to the soldiers. So Irina has been feeling alone in the house, in the 'hateful room' where Natasha has billeted her, irked by Andrei, their children and the staff, and what sound like daily visits from Protopopov. No wonder she has decided to bury her dreams – she has made her last mention of Moscow at the end of Act Three – and get married, love or no love. She explains it to Kulygin, who no doubt grasps it already:

> Well, why not? I've thought it over and decided to accept him. He's a fine man, an extraordinarily fine man . . .

All the same, something still gnaws at her:

> it's as if my heart had suddenly sprouted wings, I feel bright and cheerful, and I'm longing to get to work again . . . Only something happened yesterday, there's some sort of mystery, something's preying on my mind . . .

As if his job were to head off all possible trouble, Chebutykin makes a good joke, resourcefully reviving the word that amused Kulygin before:

> Bunkum

– and at this, by a nice coincidence, Natasha sticks her head out of the window. The news is that Olga is home. Kulygin, picking up Natasha's patronising phrase 'our headmistress', takes Irina in to greet her. As if to round off a satisfactory episode, Chebutykin returns to his newspaper and his ominous little rhyme.

*

Full of hints as it is, there is little sense that this final act will bring quite the surprises that it does. We are hearing the usual counterpoint of trivial conversation – on subjects such as Kulygin's moustache – with existential melancholy as Chebutykin looks ahead to the last stage of his life. It is all against a continuing background of general affection, which drives the company to champagne and photographs to stave off sorrow. The emotional atmosphere warms and cools, never quite settles.

As often in Chekhov, we may suddenly feel we have been with this ad hoc family almost as long as they have with each other. This is partly because of the declared passage of time, but also because we keep encountering them in subtly different settings – a name-day morning in early summer, a winter's night, another night of disruption, and now in the open air. This last, like the play in general, presents quite some challenge to the designer, working hand in hand with the director. The landscape Chekhov wants to see is described at surprising length at the start. Beyond the Prozorovs' garden, an avenue of fir trees leads to a river and woods beyond. Sometimes people are to stroll through the garden without participating in the action. It is like a painting. Much depends on the depth of the stage – and Chekhov might be surprised to know that nowadays he is performed in small theatres as well as large, sometimes with audiences surrounding the action. The minimum requirement is for a foreground where conversations take place, then a background to which characters temporarily retire but where they are still visible, and beyond that an invisible place where we imagine them continuing their business – particularly when the time comes for the fateful duel. It is an ambitious climax to the scenic pattern of the play: in the first two acts there had to be one acting area behind another; the third closed down claustrophobically to an overcrowded bedroom; and now an awesome conclusion will be played out in open space, intimate emotions against a wide landscape.

*

Two guns continue to smoke in the scene: we know that the problem between Soliony and the Baron won't go away, and

there is still no sign of Vershinin. In the background Andrei
continues to wheel his pram; in the foreground Chebutykin
sits, a still point around which the action ebbs and flows. Now
Masha approaches from background to foreground, as if the
coast is now clear and she can be alone with someone she can
really talk to. At this extreme moment for her, she and the
doctor, who normally have little to do with each other, find a
vocabulary far more explicit than anyone else in the play. It is
very direct, and not quite respectable, as if they were disrepu-
table old friends. Masha never had much taste for small talk,
but even by her standards, her new style contrasts starkly with
the evasions practised by almost everyone else. Hardly has she
sat down than she leads with a question she seems to have
waited for years to ask:

> MASHA: Were you in love with my mother?
> CHEBUTYKIN: Very much.
> MASHA: And did she love you?
> CHEBUTYKIN (*after a pause*): I don't remember.

Of course he remembers, he just won't say: in this short
moment his candour and his secretiveness are both evident.
Why does he avoid the question, and why does it take him a
pause to decide to? Is it out of delicacy, as Masha's mother was
a married woman and this after all is her daughter? Because
Masha is married too but in love with someone else? Out of
embarrassment, because his love was so one-sided? There are
plenty of decisions for the actors to make in these four brief
lines, and several good alternatives. Not the least of them is
what Masha's attitude might be to the doctor's final reply. Her
reason for asking was obvious enough: people in love only want
to talk about love, and the more dramatically agonised the
better. And finding out something of his secret makes it
possible for her to speak bluntly of her own:

> Is my man here?

So the woman who snobbishly complained about the town's
lack of culture, who wore black and whistled and recited
snatches of poetry, now sees that desire has levelled her with
'our cook Martha', who used to refer to her policeman lover as

'my man'. The term is as crude as a Prozorov can get, and she says it three times.

Of course Chebutykin knows exactly what and who she means. The play's most worldly man gives her the news she needs, with none of his usual circumlocution:

> Not yet.

The loss of Vershinin may be doing nothing for Masha's peace of mind, but it is making her extremely expressive:

> When you have to snatch your happiness in little bits, and then you lose it, as I'm doing, you become gradually coarser, you become a shrew . . . (*Points to her bosom.*) I'm seething inside, in here . . .

Within the limited language this could hardly be more erotic; and while her vision is so clear, she suddenly sees Andrei with his pram and improvises a brilliant epitaph for him:

> . . . Andrei . . . All our hopes lie in ruins. Like a great bell. It took thousands of people to raise it, at the expense of vast amounts of money and labour, then it suddenly fell down and shattered. Just like that, without rhyme or reason. That was Andrei . . .

This is a reference to the great chipped Kremlin Bell which is still visited by tourists in Moscow. Proving too difficult to hoist into place, it was simply left on the ground.

On this devastating cue, Andrei speaks at last, and does nothing to contradict Masha's judgment. Like Kulygin, he cannot escape his own obsessions, among them Natasha's life inside the house now Protopopov is here. It is certainly a good reason for him to continue to shut out the world, no longer in order to play his violin but through pure cowardice:

> Just when are we going to have some peace inside this house? It's so noisy.

It's hardly the noise that troubles him, more the human inter-actions that cause it. We take a moment to look at them all:

Andrei, Masha, Chebutykin, all of them damaged by love, their self-esteem low, their pride false, only occasionally able to call things by their names. Chebutykin, the deflection expert, now takes Andrei's 'when' literally: if it's time he is talking about, time is on the move, and as a matter of interest he has an old-fashioned timepiece which chimes on the hour – he demonstrates its action. Indeed it will strike at exactly one o'clock today, when three of the battalions are to leave town. Likewise time will move forward until tomorrow, when he will leave too – perhaps for good, perhaps not, what does it matter anyway?

This bleak and denuded prospect depresses Andrei. The distant sound of two travelling musicians with violin and harp (they will arrive shortly, so presumably we will hear them continuously from now on) underscores his impression of a world about to become meaningless without its visitors. The town will be snuffed out 'like a candle'; just as bad, he will have nothing to distract him. One of the accusations he will level at the town is its tendency to gossip; meanwhile he exemplifies it himself:

> Something happened outside the theatre last night. They're all talking about it.

With him, Chebutykin is more forthcoming: the outcome of the unpleasantness between Soliony and Tuzenbakh has been inevitable. Tuzenbakh's patience snapped, so Soliony 'had to challenge him'. What's more, time has moved on as predicted, and the critical moment looms:

> It's just about time now . . . Half-past twelve in the Crown forest.

Half an hour, that is, before the first batallion departure.

The forest is just the other side of the river, nearly visible: the audience feel they could almost witness this duel. Andrei and Masha, sunk in their own miseries, are forced to think about this new disaster. Chebutykin sums up Soliony's character as we might, his mockery now coloured with apprehension:

Bang-bang! (*Laughs.*) Soliony fancies himself as
Lermontov, even writes poetry . . . Joking aside, this'll be
his third duel.

It's clear that Chebutykin thinks nothing of the Baron's chances.
He won't even answer Masha's query as to whether Tuzenbakh has fought a duel before, and is quite brutal when she
worries that he may be in real danger: he's a 'fine chap', but:

. . . what's one Baron more or less – it hardly matters, does
it? Let them fight! Who cares?

This is quite offensive, but by now actors and audience recognise that Chebutykin is at his most cynical when he is hiding
his deepest anxieties.

There is another 'Cooo-eee! Cooo-eee!', but now it has become something to do with the duel:

CHEBUTYKIN: . . . Oh, let him wait. That's Skvortsov
shouting, one of the seconds. He's down there in the boat.

To his credit, the doctor seems in no hurry to attend the unpleasant event. And when Andrei suggests that it is a disgrace-
ful thing to fight or attend a duel, even in a medical capacity,
his familiar answer is ready and waiting, mocking Andrei's
attempts to take a moral high ground:

No, it just seems that way. We're not here, there's nothing
here, we don't exist. We only seem to exist. And what
difference does it make anyway?

Masha certainly sees this medley of nonsense for what it is:

. . . talk, talk, talk . . . (*Makes to exit.*) You live in a climate
where it snows at the drop of a hat, and on top of it all,
these stupid conversations . . .

Preoccupied as she is with Vershinin's departure – will he
come and say goodbye, or will he just vanish? – this phrasing
of hers is a little wild, like her mood, as if the likelihood of
snow made pointless talk even worse. The fact is she really
doesn't know what to do with herself. She tries to go into the

house, but the thought of Kulygin and indeed Natasha in
there is too much for her: she will continue to hang about in the
garden, hoping someone will tell her if and when Vershinin
arrives – a moment when she will hardly be able to avoid
seeing her husband as well. No wonder she envies the birds on
the wing, like Vershinin's imprisoned government minister in
Act Two:

> The birds are already migrating . . . Swans, or geese . . .
> Lucky creatures . . . (*Exits.*)

The old conspirators, Andrei and Chebutykin, are left alone.
Andrei turns from the desolation of the town to that in his
own house. He will soon be permanently 'on my own': not
literally of course, but – the next worst thing – with no Irina,
no Olga, no Masha (who will have little further reason to
visit), no soldiers or ex-soldiers:

> CHEBUTYKIN: What about your wife?

There is an interruption before Andrei replies: it does the
office of a pause. Ferapont enters with some papers, and then:

> ANDREI: My wife's my wife.

Chebutykin has the knack for making people tell the truth today. As Andrei will admit, he is:

> a friend, the only person I can open my heart to.

It is sad in itself, and not quite true: Andrei's other confidant,
Ferapont, has just come on, as always in time – so to speak –
to hear him as he unburdens himself. Andrei delivers an
epitaph on Natasha as devastating as Masha's was on him. He
reaches for the same words he thought would sustain him in
front of his sisters' screens in Act Three – Natasha is 'honest'
and 'decent' – but he can't get much further. He is not even
sure of her affability:

> she's . . . good-natured, I suppose . . .

Impatient with it all, he lets rip with what he really feels. No,
far from being honest and decent:

> there's something about her that reduces her to the level of
> some small, blind, furry animal . . . she's not human.

All the same, he can't get free of her:

> I love Natasha, I do, but at times she seems so incredibly
> vulgar, and then I'm confused.

It's a wonderful expression of muddle and dismay. The actor
has to think carefully about the ingredients. Andrei is deeply
divided, between love and disgust: what is the balance between
the two, and at what point are we to hear one turn into the
other? Is Andrei deceiving himself when he says he loves
Natasha? Has he tried to express any of this before, even to
himself? Would he free himself of his dependence if he could,
or has he settled for this quiet, unhappy life, punctuated by an
occasional complaint to a friend?

It's clear what Chebutykin thinks he should do, and it certainly has the virtue of honesty. Brutally consistent in his
belief in self-preservation at all costs, he thinks Andrei should
simply pack his bags and never come back. He stands up to
emphasise the point:

> Listen, my friend, I'm leaving tomorrow. We may never see
> each other again, so here's my advice to you. Put on your hat,
> take up your stick, and walk away . . . The further the better.

We are rather glad to hear it: it is clear-sighted and undeceived,
and perhaps not a bad idea. No one would miss Andrei much
– the children are too young to, and they would be insulated
from him by an aggrieved Natasha in any case. But it would
take quite some nerve, and Chebutykin knows his man as we
do: it (surely) won't happen.

Indeed Andrei says nothing in reply, simply standing by as
Soliony, together with his two seconds, spots Chebutykin on
his way through the garden to the rendezvous in the forest. It
is half past twelve, and Soliony is brisk and prepared, to
Chebutykin's disgust:

> I'm fed up with all of you (*To Andrei.*) Andrei, dear chap, if
> anyone's looking for me, tell them I'll be back presently . . .
> (*Sighs.*) Oh dear.

Apparently all too sure of himself, Soliony repeats his disruptive Krylov fable about the bear. Then he inappropriately asks after the doctor's own health, before promising he won't kill the Baron, but only, as the better marksman, 'wing him, like a woodcock'. But we know that Soliony too has his defences: spouting bursts of poetry may be covering up a certain nervousness. Also, his hands 'smell like a corpse' – whereupon he quotes again, this time from his hero Lermontov. But this time it doesn't work: Chebutykin trumps him by repeating the Krylov, as if that was his last word on the business in hand:

> 'Before he had time to gasp, the bear had him in its grasp . . .'

They leave, to the increasingly ominous 'Coo-eee!'. First it was Rodé genially testing the echo; then an unattributed sound from the far end of the garden; then a call from one of the seconds; now it rings out to summon the duellists to their destiny.

On top of it, like a chilling grace note, comes what sounds like the cry of a lost bird – Kulygin, crossing the stage in search of his wife, as he so often is. Amongst these sounds there has been a short bustle of fruitless pursuit: Andrei has arrived with Ferapont after him but immediately escaped offstage, while Ferapont retired to the middle distance to wait patiently for his next opportunity. Irina and Tuzenbakh have arrived at the same time as Kulygin, so his rapid exit leaves them alone.

*

One of the highlights of this section of the play is when we glimpse a possible reason for Chebutykin's spiritual darkness. The trail runs back to Act One, when his first words to Irina were:

> My dear sweet child . . . My little white bird . . .

Soon afterwards he justified his gift of a samovar by saying that he had known her since the day she was born and had loved her mother. This was intriguing but no more. Then, in Act Three, at the very moment that Irina reiterated that she herself, as well as the army, would be leaving, Chebutykin dropped and broke her mother's clock, either by accident or design. Now he has reacted to her plans to start a new life, leaving him like a bird too old to fly, with, for him, exceptional feeling. Does he remember Irina's mother with tenderness, with grief, or even a degree of vengefulness (hence the dropping of the clock)? And – a large thought – if Mrs Prozorov loved him back, we realise that there is a hint, just a hint, that he might be Irina's father.

This is something Chekhov does quite often: to let an idea flit through the air, unelaborated – a hidden story, a scandal, a secret connection between the characters. In *The Seagull* too, there is a hint of an unacknowledged paternity. Interestingly enough (unlike a less self-confident writer), Chekhov seems to feel no need to settle the matter, so that it remains as deep a secret for the audience as for the characters.

*

Tuzenbakh is improbably dressed for his duel in a straw hat, which hardly inspires confidence. Perhaps it is his attempt to throw Irina off the scent. We are seeing the two of them for the first time since their life together was settled, so are interested to know how candid they will be with each other – about Kulygin's latest panic, for instance, which they can hardly ignore:

> TUZENBAKH: I think he's the only person in the town who's glad the army's leaving.
>
> IRINA: That's understandable.
> *A pause.*

So whatever their new intimacy, it doesn't stretch to a real discussion of Masha's scandal. Instead, Irina broadens the subject to the effect of the army's departure on all of them:

> The town'll be empty now.

The conversation stalls at this obvious point, the question of where Tuzenbakh is about to go this morning becoming unavoidable. In fact he is trying to find a way of following Soliony across the river, while protecting Irina from worry: he hopes she has no inkling of the duel. His excuse is quite feeble – he has to go 'into town' to see his army colleagues off. Irina sees right through this, and uses his familiar name to get him to own up to her:

Nikolai, why are you so distracted today?
A pause.
What happened outside the theatre?

Tuzenbakh has already waved this subject aside once, in front of Kulygin and Chebutykin. Likewise, he prefers now to dwell on his love for Irina. It may be in his mind that, if things go badly for him and he is not 'back within the hour, by your side', these are the last words she will remember:

My dearest darling . . . (*Gazing into her eyes.*) You know, five years have gone by, since I fell in love with you, and I still can't get used to it. You grow more beautiful every day.

The truth surely is that she has grown older, her natural optimism more and more dampened by experience, but he sees only the hair and eyes he has always loved. Nothing can compromise his devotion or his hope:

And tomorrow I'll take you away, and we'll work, we'll be rich, all my dreams will come true.

Still, he is not quite at his best: riches he doesn't need – that wasn't the point of working – and he is speaking only of the beauty of her face now, not her spirit. Something is in the way, and he can't escape the awful drawback, like a brick wall before his face:

There's only one thing, just one: you don't love me.

Irina, to her credit (but our alarm, since we know these may be her last words to him), repays his honesty:

There's nothing I can do about that. I'll be your wife, I'll be faithful and obedient, but I don't love you. I can't help it.

Unlike Masha, who once deceived herself she was in love with Kulygin, and Olga, who would even marry an old man in return for kindness, Irina is unappeasably honest. A great love was always her dream, and though she came to the point of calling it nonsense, it is still an unanswered call in her. Without it:

> it's as if my heart were a valuable grand piano, which someone's locked up, and they've lost the key.

It must be devastating for Tuzenbakh to hear: there is a pause for his reaction:

> IRINA: You look worried.

Yes indeed, but evasiveness runs side by side with his painful honesty. As we can well imagine, he has had no rest, but he tells her only part of the reason, pretending there is no worry in his life but one:

> that lost key tears me apart, it won't let me sleep . . .

Having broken into his night, it's ruining his waking hours; he can't bear to leave things as they are, and a rawer, more primitive voice bursts out of him:

> Speak to me, Irina.
> *A pause.*
> Say something . . .

But she can't. The only comfort she can give him is to rest her head on his chest and share what she sees – an ancient landscape longer-lived than them and now seeming to hold its breath:

> Everything around us is so mysterious, the old trees stand silently . . .

Tuzenbakh needs more than this, and he can't let it go – what follows could almost be a quarrel were it not for their affection:

> TUZENBAKH: Speak to me, say anything . . .
> IRINA: What can I say?
> TUZENBAKH: Anything.
> IRINA: Don't, please!

Irina can never have heard him talk like this before, or known him to be at such a loss: of all people he has never been short of a speech, or less than reassuring. Now there is nothing but blank need.

A pause allows their feelings to settle a little. In his roundabout way, Tuzenbakh starts to philosophise; but really he is asking for the small verbal reassurances any lover needs, the very ones Irina can't give him:

> it's strange how the silliest things in life can suddenly seem so important, for no particular reason. You laugh at them the same as always, you can see them for the trivial things they are, but you carry on regardless, as if you hadn't the power to stop.

He concludes that the best thing would be not to speak about 'that' any more; preferable, now he is on a philosophical plane, to stay there. His ability to talk could be his salvation, in fact. He suddenly feels 'elated', rather as Irina did when she passed her exams; he seems to be seeing everything, 'these fir-trees, and maples and birches', for the first time. If such trees are beautiful, then life should be beautiful. It is the familiar, enlarging effect of falling in love, but at the same time it suggests someone on the scaffold, saying goodbye to life. As if in confirmation, that sinister 'Cooo-eee!' rings out once more. Then Tuzenbakh's true need to identify with nature is explained – there is a dead tree there, but it still sways with the others as if it were alive. So it may be for him:

> I think if I die, I'll still be a part of life, come what may. Goodbye, my darling . . .

Irina can hardly miss the meaning of this. He realises he may have let the cat out of the bag, and immediately comforts her with a domestic detail:

> Oh, those papers you gave me are lying on my desk, under the calendar.

Undeceived, she suddenly determines to come with him, wherever:

IRINA: I'm coming with you.
TUZENBAKH (*hastily*): No, no

– and before she can do it, he wards her off, most poignantly.
He starts to leave but stops, instinctively looking to assure her
(if not himself) that he will be back soon enough:

TUZENBAKH: Irina . . .
IRINA: Yes?

But he hasn't rehearsed the next part. His stopping was really
a need for comfort at the last minute – the solace of her
company, the pleasure of a morning drink. For a moment he
sounds like the husband he hopes he will be spared to be:

TUZENBAKH (*unsure what to say*): I haven't had coffee yet.
Ask them to make some, will you? (*Hurriedly exits.*)

*

It is impossible, in this short and heartbreaking scene, not to
feel Chekhov's wisdom and perception of human behaviour. It
may be gently expressed, but his vision of our separateness
from each other is bleak and undeceived. The scene is likely to
bring the best from any sensitive actors, once they have settled
certain basic questions, such as what Irina knows in her bones
about the duel, and how much her fiancé senses that she
knows. This balance between what is withheld on Tuzenbakh's
part and guessed at on Irina's dictates his over-protectiveness,
and, by contrast, her refusal to equivocate about her feelings,
or lack of them. The audience should be deeply affected by
Tuzenbakh's desperation, exposed and then covered up; his
desire for reassurance balked by her honesty; the self-imposed
solitude in which such an honesty leaves her. A wealth of
unspoken feeling, contradictory and turbulent, lies beneath
the couple's simple, affectionate exchanges.

*

The barely suppressed emotions of this scene have built up a
pressure like water behind a dam: Andrei now returns with his
pram, vainly pursued by Ferapont, and in full flood. It may

have been his sudden honesty a few moments ago with Chebutykin that causes his outburst now: with no more temporising, he must shout the truth at the top of his voice. Not only for him, but for the play itself, with its gathering sense of tragedy, this comes at exactly the right moment. Everything he began to admit in his sisters' bedroom is broadcast: he is as eloquent as Irina was in the same scene, but more bitterly turned on himself:

> Oh, where is it now, where's my past gone, eh? . . . Why is it we become so dull, grey and uninteresting, when we've barely started to live?

Unlike Irina, he is also turning on the society that has corrupted him:

> This town's been in existence now for two hundred years, with a hundred thousand inhabitants, and there isn't one of them any different from the rest, not a single great man, alive or dead.

He and they are almost indistinguishable – it is people like him who have failed the community, but the community has also crushed his 'dreams and clever ideas', poisoned the soil in which an exceptional artist or scientist could survive:

> All they do is eat, drink, sleep and eventually die . . .
> Others are born, and they too eat, drink, sleep, and so as not to die of boredom, bring some variety into their lives with vicious backbiting, vodka, gambling and lawsuits.

The two threads of his anger finally merge, his own story identical with all others:

> Wives betray their husbands, and the husbands lie, and pretend they see nothing, hear nothing, while their vulgarity irresistibly influences the children, crushes the life out of them, extinguishes the divine spark . . .

For the actor, the extremity of Andrei's emotion is obvious enough, but it is quite difficult to decide how to focus it. As with the 'soliloquies' in Act Three, Andrei seems to be addressing the audience; but present too are the eternal Ferapont, and at a distance Andrei's youngest sister, also close to despair and awaiting her fate, sitting on a swing, lost in thought. If Andrei includes them and they can hear him, they will have to respond, albeit without lines; if he speaks only to the audience, he is providing them with an unusual editorial comment they may even imagine to be Chekhov's main point. And as for the pitch of it, though I said Andrei was shouting, this may not be literally true: he could equally well speak quietly, introspectively, his self-reproach all the more deadly for its calmness. In either version, we may well remember it as, paradoxically, his finest moment.

In any case, there is no escaping Ferapont, limited witness to everything, provider of useless information:

> FERAPONT: . . . These papers have to be signed.
> ANDREI: You're getting on my nerves.
> FERAPONT (*hands over the papers*): The porter at the finance office was telling me just now . . . he says, last winter in St Petersburg they had two hundred degrees of frost.

Ferapont's gossip is of the harmless kind, compared to what Andrei has just castigated. But its very naiveté takes Andrei round an emotional hairpin bend, rather as the decision to marry took Irina, and the possibility of death did Tuzenbakh:

> I detest the life I lead now, but when I think about the future, well, that's something else! Everything seems so airy and bright . . .

In this volatile moment, his despair flipping over into blind optimism, Andrei sounds like Vershinin and Tuzenbakh philosophising in happier days. No longer crushed by their elders' vulgarity, his children are suddenly to be:

> free from idleness, from perpetual stale beer, and goose and cabbage, from after-dinner naps, from all this vulgar dependency . . .

The dramatic mood swing is typical of most of these characters – it is tempting to say it is typically Russian – but not of

Ferapont. By comic contrast he is immovable, except to say that it might have been Moscow, not Petersburg, that had had the frost. Again he seems to affect Andrei by simply uttering; his emotion, as it did at the end of Act Three, boils down to its simplest ingredient:

> Oh, my dear sisters, my darling sisters! (*Tearfully.*) Dearest Masha . . .

Why only Masha, the actor might ask – is she by chance the first to come to mind, or is it because deep down Andrei knows she is a fellow-sufferer? Would he go on to name the other sisters, were it not for the inevitable interruption from inside the house, from the self-inflicted cause of so many of his woes?

> NATASHA (*at the window*): Who's making all that noise out here? Is it you, Andrei? You'll waken Sophie. *Il ne faut pas faire de bruit, la Sophie est dormée déjà. Vous êtes un ours.*

Chekhov couldn't resist it, this final display of heartless vulgarity from her. For one thing, if Natasha's French were better, she would have said 'est endormée'. It's the second time she has used the word 'déjà' wrongly; and Sophie should not have been given the definite article.

Andrei is now further emasculated as father and husband: Natasha insists that he give up the pram with the precious Sophie (who doesn't in fact seem to have woken up) to old Ferapont, a better guardian. This is when we might long for him to give her a piece of his mind, especially in his present mood; but all he can manage – no better than Olga defending Anfisa in the previous act – is:

> (*Embarrassed.*) I was talking quietly.

Anyway, Natasha isn't listening: she has moved on to the next thing, standing in her window holding Bobik as if posing for a portrait:

> Bobik! Naughty Bobik! Who's a little rascal?

Not as seriously naughty, it seems, as her little husband.

There is nothing Andrei can do to break into this. The scene settles again as he signs his papers, sustained by Natasha's gently remorseless burbling: you could almost wish Soliony were here to insult her.

A few minutes ago, as Masha spoke of her new shrewishness, a violin and a portable harp were faintly heard in the distance. Now the players, a man and a girl, pass through the garden, pausing long enough to be heard by Vershinin, Olga and Anfisa, who come out of the house. They are joined by Irina, approaching from her swing. Olga seems none too pleased: it is not so long since her bedroom likewise became 'like a public thoroughfare'. In view of her essential good nature, this irritation suggests quite a degree of anxiety. Beside her is Vershinin, who could be the cause of it, and the long-suffering Anfisa, whose luck seems to have changed in a most unexpected way – in fact she could be the one person hereabouts who has benefited from events. She has indeed moved out of the house, as Natasha would wish, but as she explains:

> What a life I have! I'm living in a school flat now with my lovely Olya – that's what the good Lord's granted me in my old age.

She has a room and bed of her own there, and since the flat belongs to the school, she has no rent to pay either. No wonder, being who she is, that she is sensitive to the less fortunate musicians, compelled to go from house to house in search of tips, and she gives them money, Olga's presumably:

> Poor things. You don't have to play round the streets if you're well fed.

Natasha's hostility has turned out to be a tremendous blessing in disguise:

> It's a big flat . . . I wake up at night sometimes, and I think, oh, Holy Mother of God, I must be the happiest person in the world!

This little part of the story might seem unimportant, but it illustrates a significant theme: that it is possible to survive against bad odds. At a time when everybody is having to adapt to changed circumstances (as all Russians would soon have to), the oldest (and most religious) character, apparently most trapped in her peasant past, has been the most successful. And her response to the less fortunate is in steep contrast with Natasha's self-conscious remarks about the 'obligations' of the rich which she had to listen to during the fire.

Though there is a continuing sense of one crisis on the heels of another, the pleasure of this moment makes us forget what remains to be settled. If the production is working well, Anfisa and Andrei will have put the great matter of Vershinin's and Masha's parting out of mind. But now we see how stuck Vershinin is in the mechanics of what he has to do. If he is to say goodbye to Masha properly, they need to be alone, yet here are her two sisters and the jubilant Anfisa. He can only drop an obvious hint, glancing at his watch:

> We' ll be leaving soon, Olga. It's time I was going.
> *A pause.*
> I wish you all the very best . . . Where's Masha?
> IRINA: She's in the garden somewhere . . . I'll go and find her.

Irina knows the significance of this, of course; whether Anfisa does or not, she goes off with Irina, calling her own, homely version of 'Coo-eee!'. Olga and Vershinin are left there, the lover and the sister. It is awkward. Their loyalties may be at odds. Perhaps Olga knows little more than the audience about Vershinin's real feelings for Masha; it comes to the same in any case, since he is certainly leaving. This being the least blunt of families, the air is especially thick with things unspoken. Vershinin marks time:

> Well, all good things come to an end . . .

He means the soldiers' visit, but of course there is a second meaning in it, to do with Masha: it is as if he were delivering a warning. He makes more small talk, explaining how he has had to attend an official lunch with the Mayor of the town, but how during all the champagne and speeches his mind:

was elsewhere – here, with all of you. (*Looks around the garden.*) Yes, I've got so used to you.

He may not quite mean 'all of you': his inner thought is betrayed by that involuntary look round the garden.

Will they ever meet again? Olga wonders, as Irina did at the start of the scene. Vershinin is as realistic as Fedotik was:

Probably not.

So there, in conversational code, is the depth of Masha's plight – this goodbye really will be final. A few ruthlessly practical arrangements: Olga will keep an eye on Vershinin's family until they follow him in a month or two, and alert him to any trouble. This will hardly be enjoyable for her: it will add to the strangeness of the town with everyone gone. She opens up a little, to ease the situation:

Nothing ever turns out the way we'd like.

Since they are all embarking on a new and unexpected life, she wants Vershinin to understand that change always involves disappointment. She never intended to be a headmistress, though she is one (just as Natasha insisted), and that means she won't ever get back to Moscow – simple. She is giving Vershinin the chance to speak a little more openly, but he doesn't really rise to it. He stumbles:

Anyway . . . Thank you for everything . . . I'm sorry if there's anything I've done . . . I've talked a lot, I know – far too much. Forgive me for that, and don't think ill of me . . .

He is still in code, of course: if he needs forgiveness, it's not for the talking. Olga has to wipe her eyes – perhaps because he is failing, perhaps because she hears his real meaning; its true hopelessness for Masha.

Vershinin now begins talking all over again, almost in a parody of himself: he wants her to know that life now seems 'hopelessly dreary' but 'it's gradually getting easier, and clearer', and soon 'it'll shine out like a beacon'. But he can't keep that up either:

(*Looks at his watch.*) I really ought to be going.

He has another try: war is a thing of the past, and now there is a void to be filled:

Mankind is passionately searching for something, though, and we shall find it.

He becomes almost incoherent with the effort of keeping on with this stuff while his mind is full of something else:

If we could only find a way of injecting some culture into work, and some hard work into culture!

It is almost unbearable – and, in the true Chekhov manner, so entirely true to life that it is even a little funny. Will Masha never arrive, after all her prowling in the garden and waiting?

Suddenly, there she is. Vershinin can only state the obvious:

I've come to say goodbye

– while Olga 'walks a little way apart, so as not to inhibit the leavetaking'. Chekhov, almost directing the scene, goes on to specify that Masha gazes into Vershinin's eyes, but she says nothing apart from a single word, like the polite response of a stranger:

Goodbye.

But the next moment she is in his arms, kissing him at length, holding him, weeping. It is an extraordinary moment in the play: after nearly four acts of suppressed emotion, the most passionate physical contact. Olga for one cannot bear the candour of it:

Stop it, stop . . .

For her this is a time for self-control, not surrender. But Masha 'sobs bitterly', and Vershinin makes a minimal attempt at the commonplace:

Write to me . . . Don't forget!

He can manage nothing further, suddenly overwhelmed by the need to get away from her and on his way, to breathe free if regretful air:

Please, let me go, it's time . . .

He appeals to the older sister, as if Masha were a baby:

Olga, take her, please, I have to go . . . I'm late . . .

Heaven forbid that he, the commanding officer, should be late. 'Deeply moved' in one way or another, he kisses Olga's hand, embraces Masha once again and hurries off.

So after all that, it was over in a second – there could hardly have been fewer words. The parting that was unavoidable since Masha encouraged Vershinin to sit and look at her face where the light was brighter has been and gone. Inevitably we continue to wonder about Vershinin's feelings; the question has never really gone away. He is 'deeply moved', says Chekhov, but it is also possible that he has been in this situation before, perhaps more than once, and been 'deeply moved' each time. Is he a serial lover who always moves on, or was this unusual, even unprecedented? There is absolutely no sign given: the actor will have to decide for himself, but probably allow his true emotions to remain veiled.

Unlike Masha's: we watch her spiralling into blackness without him. At least she has Olga; but within a moment, Kulygin is standing where Vershinin did, unable to wait any longer, and having presumably observed the parting from inside the house. His immediate attentiveness to his wife could be played either as a courageous act or a possessive one. He doesn't shirk the moment; but something in his tone hints that he assumes she is weeping out of guilt about him rather than love of Vershinin:

. . . my dear, good Masha . . . You're my wife, and I'm happy, no matter what . . . I'm not complaining, I wouldn't dream of reproaching you . . . not a hint of blame . . .

On the other hand, this may simply be an easier thing for him to articulate than its humiliating alternative. What he promises we sense will come true: Masha can look forward now to a life of determined understanding from a man she no longer loves at all. At the moment it is entirely irrelevant to her, and she speaks in an opposite register, almost a different language. Her quotation is, as it was at the start of the play, from Pushkin's *Ruslan and Lyudmila*:

> 'By a curving shore stands a green oak tree, bound with a golden chain . . . bound with a golden chain . . . ' I'm going mad . . .

As the poem was familiar to all Russians, this is like muttering a comforting piece of Shakespeare or the lyric of a well-known song to get yourself out of trouble. It only helps a little: she can get no further than that golden chain, just as she couldn't before. However she gradually seems to calm down. As Vershinin moves that bit further away, so do her tears – proof, in Kulygin's eyes, that she is 'a good woman'.

The story unfurls relentlessly, indifferent to her: at this worst of moments we hear 'the muffled sound of a shot'. We had forgotten, and Irina, hurrying up to help in the new crisis, isn't putting two and two together. The duel is done, but no one seems to notice, because they don't know of any duel, though Irina must suspect it. Masha continues to settle, adding a green cat into her Pushkin. This is not as mad as it sounds: there is a learned cat in the next part of the poem, though it is not green, so she is no more than 'mixed up'. Neither Olga nor Irina, in this unfamiliar trouble, can do much except wait and soothe. Irina believes they should all sit quietly together and talk about her departure the next day; Olga thinks salvation lies inside the house. There is, in other words, no way they can approach the actual problem. Any kind of enclosure indoors, particularly with Natasha there, is horrible for Masha; just as she preferred to watch the swans and geese flying away while waiting for Vershinin, she will be better off now roaming the garden like an animal:

> (*Angrily.*) I'm not going in there. (*Begins sobbing, but stops almost immediately.*) I don't go in there any more . . .

Her husband then does a remarkable thing, inspired in its way. He who has recently shaved himself whips out a false beard and moustache that he has confiscated from one of his pupils. Presumably he has kept it for exactly such a moment, when a joke just might help:

> I look like our German teacher, don't you think? (*Laughs.*)
> They're so funny, those boys.

If his first effort at forgiveness was misjudged, this gamble with Masha's feelings, a reminder of their everyday life, is generous to her. And generous too to his pupils, whom he has never spoken of with affection before. It works:

> MASHA: Actually, you do look like the German teacher.
> OLGA (*laughs*): Yes, you do.

But only for a moment; then:

> *Masha starts crying.*

– and all Kulygin can do is to repeat, defeated:

> Just like him.

Natasha seems to have an instinct for interrupting at the worst moment, her pettiness colliding with the powerful emotions of others – she lives in a different world, oblivious. At first she fails to notice Kulygin's beard and moustache: she is too involved in issuing instructions to the maid. From these we learn that Sophie, passed on from Natasha's husband to Ferapont, is now to be under the care of the sinister Protopopov. We wonder fleetingly whether he might be her true father – a reasonable enough supposition that, as with Chebutykin and Irina, Chekhov will never confirm. As for Andrei, as Bobik's undisputed father he can take care of him. For now, Irina seems to be Natasha's main focus, though she does break off to complain of the 'fright' Kulygin's disguise has given her. In a group of people desperately reacting to change, her response is unvaryingly selfish:

> Irina, you're leaving tomorrow – what a shame . . . You
> know, I've got so used to you, it's not going to be easy to say
> goodbye to you, believe me.

To say that she has 'grown used' to the person whose house this actually is shows she has lost little of her nerve.

Irina's imminent departure has obliged Natasha to do a whole lot more rearranging: now Andrei must go into Irina's room (presumably the one she was sharing with Olga), and Sophie will have Andrei's presumably quite large room (larger than she needs) to herself. It is a sort of chaos. Having possibly admitted the truth – 'children are such a bother' – to her maid, Natasha finds it necessary to boast to her equals about Sophie, just as she did about Bobik in Act Two. It is her habitual defence against criticism:

> She's such a delightful child, an absolute angel.

If only Soliony were there to fry Sophie in a frying-pan along with Bobik, but he of course is busy frying the Baron. Kulygin, ever-helpful and trying to see the best in everything just now, has to agree:

> She's a beautiful child, that's true.

– he who presumably has no hope of becoming a father.

The one thing Natasha always does for the good is to unite everyone else against her. Whatever the stresses between Masha, her sisters and Kulygin, they can at least agree on this. They stand there united as she returns to her favourite topic, herself:

> So, tomorrow I'll be on my own. (*Sighs.*)

(Andrei obviously doesn't count, or the children, or Protopopov.)

She continues to outline the future. Best to keep loneliness at bay with some landscape gardening – the fir-trees and maples that Tuzenbakh found such a feeling for had better come down; highly scented flowers planted by humans 'for the per- fume' will take the place of nature. Superbly, in the midst of this and almost as an aside, she even finds an opportunity to insult Irina precisely the way Olga once took Natasha to task:

> Really, my dear, that sash doesn't suit you at all . . . It looks awful . . .

The worm has indeed turned. And to complete the impression that this may be the last we see of her, she concludes with essence of Natasha, as violent as when she stamped her foot over Anfisa in Olga's bedroom:

> What's this fork doing on the bench? (*Walks up to the house, shouting to the maid.*) I want to know – what's this fork doing on the bench! (*Shrieks.*) Shut up!

And so we take our leave of a most uncongenial character. But Natasha has not set out to be dislikeable: the line about the sash is a nasty one, to be sure, but she is only taking an obvious revenge, exactly tit-for-tat. If it were the other way round, a retaliatory remark by one of the sisters, we would probably applaud it. And it brings out the best in Kulygin, a moment of untypical dry wit:

> KULYGIN: She's off again.

There is a final question still unanswered. It was raised by the shot that rang out, followed now by another sound, a military band accompanyng the soldiers on their way. Will Soliony be among them? Vershinin certainly is. Again Masha refers to his kind as Martha the cook might have done:

> Our men are leaving. Well . . . *Bon voyage* to them!

After so much emotion, blank domesticity seems to be closing the story:

> MASHA (*to Kulygin*): We'd better go home . . . Where's my hat and cape?
> KULYGIN: I took them inside . . . I'll go and fetch them.

But just as the company seem to be disbanding, Chebutykin is among them like a ghost, trying to catch Olga on her own and unobserved:

> OLGA: What is it? (*Pause.*) What's the matter?
> CHEBUTYKIN: Nothing . . . I don't know how to tell you . . . (*Whispers in her ear.*)

Of course the worst has happened, and the old man doesn't yet have the courage to say it out loud. As Olga reacts with horror, he retreats to his favourite position:

> I've had enough, I'm sick of it all . . . I don't want to talk about it . . . (*Testily.*) Anyway, what does it matter?

Then it is Olga who cannot speak, but only hold Irina in her arms and repeat Chebutykin's phrase:

> . . . I don't know how to tell you . . .

And at last the old doctor, having convinced himself of the unimportance of his news, tosses it into the group like some irrelevant anecdote from his paper:

> The Baron's been killed in a duel . . .

And sure enough, his newspaper will be out in a moment and he out of sight behind it – Chebutykin, who saw it all and, as the doctor on hand, presumably pronounced Tuzenbakh wounded beyond recovery. In case we should be in any doubt of it, he signals his detachment from the whole 'nasty business' with his saucy song:

> 'Ta-ra-ra boom-dee-ay, ta-ra-ra boom-dee-ay.'

So this is why Soliony laid plans to leave by boat, unlike his colleagues: if he were to win the duel and kill or wound Tuzenbakh, he would hardly want to come back to this house for farewells.

Irina's grief is quiet, as it often is:

> Oh, I knew it, I knew it . . .

Chekhov himself commented cynically on this in a letter:

> When a woman guesses something she always says 'I knew it, I knew it.'

But there is little doubt of what we will feel. Irina has, in a moment, lost everything – a husband, a future that might have realised some of her dreams. Most terrible of all, he went to his death knowing that she didn't love him: in her honesty she couldn't pretend she did. She sensed in her bones where he must be going, and failed to go with him or to keep him here. If the grief weren't enough, her lingering sense of responsibility will make it nearly unbearable.

There is nothing for the sisters to do but hold on to each other, and they form a classic portrait of isolation and mutual dependence:

> *The three sisters are standing with their arms around each other.*

As they do so, and without compromising the humanity of their feelings, the play changes its nature a little. In its final moments it forms a summary without losing its power. Each sister speaks in turn, not exactly of what has happened but of her determination to survive it. As Tuzenbakh predicted – and as he and Vershinin felt their way towards expressing – they experience the human need not to be forgotten, for their lives to have final meaning. For Masha, the music of the band marks the loss of her man, of Irina's, and of all their recent friends. Nevertheless it is time:

> to begin life over again.

– and so she will, blighted as her life seems:

> We must live . . . we must . . .

For Irina, a day will come, beyond death perhaps, when human confusion and suffering will be understood and there will 'be no more mysteries'; for now, she will continue with the life she planned with Tuzenbakh and become the play's third schoolteacher, in order:

> to devote my whole life to people who need it.

So the familiar theme rings out again:

> I'll be working . . . yes, working.

For Olga, the eldest, suffering is less dramatic – she is the least directly affected – but perhaps lifelong. Her task now is to take charge and sum up, having had a few moments to find the strength for it while the others spoke. As the band plays the brigade out of town, she brings the women of her family together. One day their pain will be understood and even enrich the lives of others:

> . . . I want to live so much! . . . Time will pass, and we'll be gone forever, we'll be forgotten . . . But our sufferings will turn to joy for those who come after us . . .

Within this generosity, she finds a degree of hope: relief will come sooner than that. She convinces herself for a moment that one day they will themselves know why they have endured all this:

> . . . my dear sisters . . . We must live! The band plays on so cheerfully, so joyously – it's as if any minute now we'll discover why we live, why we suffer . . . Oh, if only we knew! If only we knew!

The effort she needs to create even the beginnings of this fragile confidence is heroic. It is beside the point that there is a deal of self-deception in it, and that she is the least logical of the three speakers. As when Andrei found a final moment of hope, it is not a matter of objective truth, but of finding some idea to draw strength from. This is what the sisters have always done, first by fixing their thoughts on Moscow and now on paradise ahead; perhaps, after all, to do such a thing is a human necessity.

Stanislavsky's plan for the original Moscow Art Theatre production was to add to this final tableau the sight of Tuzenbakh's body being carried across the rear of the stage, but Chekhov wisely vetoed it. He wanted to see just what he'd written. So to complete the play's final photograph, Kulygin arrives with Masha's coat, 'in high spirits' now the soldiers are gone: it is hard to imagine how things will be for the two of them once they get home, but somehow life will continue. Andrei passes, with Bobik in the pram now. His survival will be simply a matter of keeping going with the children, with Natasha and her lover, but at least he will from time to time feel the strength of articulated anger. Chebutykin questions, for the third time since he arrived with the bad news, whether any of it matters anyway: in a further show of indifference, he continues to mutter: 'Ta-ra-ra boom-dee-ay, I'm sitting by the road today'. He may come back next year, unless he can manage to die before then. Everyone, for the time being or for good, will go on – even he. Olga is given the last word, straining to get past the limits of her knowledge. She repeats what she has just said – perhaps more upbeat this time, perhaps less, or, more probably, as the simplest of re-statements:

Oh, if only we knew! If only we knew!

Although Chekhov commented disparagingly that the end of this play was the same as that of *Uncle Vanya*, the effect of its carefully interwoven disasters and losses is profoundly moving in the theatre. There has been a community of emotion: we have felt for the suffering of everyone except possibly Natasha, who seems incapable of such a thing. Even Soliony, nervously playing with his scent bottle, had his moment. Vershinin's almost mute parting from Masha was heartbreaking, but so, unexpectedly, were Kulygin's efforts to amuse her with his false whiskers. And though the play has continually made fun of illusions, some kind of belief in a better future has prevailed as a stark necessity – whether it is the ambition of the sisters, or the limited determination of Kulygin, and even Chebutykin, to wake up to another day. The devastated Prozorovs will take up their burdens, and, looking to many people like leftovers from another era, step into a future of small efforts and modest hopes. Poised on the edge of Russia's upheaval, in all their vulnerability, feebleness but final courage, they begin to fade into history as we watch – to be forgotten by it perhaps, but not by us.

The Characters

THE RESIDENTS

FYODOR ILYICH KULYGIN

(FyAWDor EelyEETCH KoolEEghin)

The extraordinary character of Kulygin, schoolteacher and one of the play's two betrayed husbands, is to some extent (like that of Natasha) set up comically – Chekhov always enjoyed making fun of pedagogues, at least the male ones. His arrival in the play – making a great speech about himself and the occasion, recommending taking up the carpets, brandishing a gift for Irina that he has already given her at Easter and proclaiming his personal happiness – is preposterously cheerful.

This happiness is obviously not shared by Masha, his wife. It is surprising, in a way, that he needs a wife at all; so embedded is he in the life of a provincial boys' school, completely in thrall to his headmaster – a character we are probably relieved not to meet. Kulygin's only need for a wife is to have someone to share his professional worries and to show off on public occasions – though the uncooperative Masha is probably becoming more and more of a liability in that respect. As soon as we realise this, we see how much of a mask he is wearing.

By the time the play opens, his possessive jollity, his anxious attempts to isolate Masha from the rest of her family, the interminable visits to his colleagues (even on the day of rest, as in the first act), are conspiring to drive her mad and prepare her for Vershinin. But among the things we need to sense about Kulygin in performance is why Masha was originally attracted to him. She married him soon after leaving school, at eighteen, young and inexperienced certainly, but there must have been something reassuringly paternal in his good nature and brainy self-confidence. He seems to be a good teacher, and his kindness is acknowledged by Irina. He is certainly a professional, well able to see that Irina's pretensions later to the same job may be a lot of hot air. The bitter truth, as with some marriages, is not so much that it was always a wrong choice, but that it has become one with time. By now Masha is unforgiving, and Kulygin presumably does not understand why the adoring girl he married has become so harshly un-accommodating, so mocking of the very things in him that used to charm her. He can only deal with this disillusion by ignoring it, or pretending her cutting comments are a joke. He insists ever more stridently that he is 'very, very happy', which of course he would not do if he were, and above all he never openly reproaches her, apart from awarding her a C-minus for conduct when she threatens to get drunk at lunch. The worst thing he will ever say of Masha is that Irina has a 'gentler nature' – but he quickly qualifies even that by pointing out that Masha has 'a very nice nature too'. He holds on to her through thick and thin by means of the most determined toleration, with a tenacity not unlike Natasha's, his fellow-resident in the town. His unlimited capacity for putting up with things could be seen as evidence of the dignity that can be achieved within a failing relationship – or as the most desperate attempt not to lose face: Masha has to stay on his arm, even if he has to chain her to it.

Even more than with the other characters, the truth about Kulygin is always hidden, covered by his armoury of behavioural devices. Although we cannot doubt his feelings as he watches his wife disappear into Vershinin's arms, they are only suggested by indirect details; a little too much curiosity in Act Two as to where she is and why Protopopov is hanging around outside; slightly too many appearances in the room to find her in Act Three; and in the last act, an agonised clowning as he wears a false beard and moustache confiscated from one of his pupils. At this stage, his pain is also brilliantly suggested by Chekhov through his greater emotionalism overall, and through the display of a certain general kindness that has always been in him. His common humanity, his sense of himself as part of the great Russian family, makes him afraid that the departure of Fedotik and Rodé (members of a regiment that he desperately wants gone from the town) will make him weep; for him they are yet another kind of loss.

As a final way of encoding his feelings, the Latin tags he chooses to employ are significant. In Act One, one of them translates that he has done all he can, and more powerful men must do better things; in Act Two he comments on the vanity of human wishes; in Act Three he admits he carries everything he owns, his whole identity, with him. By Act Four he seems to draw no more consolation from such proverbs, though he drops a couple of more commonplace ones into his conversation. As he stands, his false beard at the ready, humiliated and cuckolded while his wife sobs her heart out over Vershinin, but determined that life shall go on, we cannot but extend the same sympathy to him as to her and see that despite his less appealing qualities, he is a fully-rounded figure in all his complexity and struggle.

NATASHA

(NatAHsha)

We know nothing about Natasha's family or where she comes from, except that she is 'local'; so, for the more upper-class sisters (despite the fact that after eleven years they are locals themselves), she might as well dwell in outer darkness. The barrier between residents and 'incomers' in Chekhov can be, as in life, ineradicable. Unlike the sisters and like Kulygin, you cannot imagine Natasha anywhere else; not only does she belong here, but she is intent on sinking her roots deeper and deeper, to support her upward mobility.

I – and the actress playing her – keep trying to make a case for her, since that is what all characterisation in the theatre demands. It is certainly easier to make one against her: she is very harshly judged by commentators on the play, even described as a 'devil of destruction'. You can see why. At the start, there is something exaggerated about her constant pleas of being unused to company and therefore 'terribly awkward' – it is a surefire way of attracting Andrei's protectiveness. From being out of her depth with the Prozorovs, she proceeds to drown them one by one – Andrei obviously, while Irina and Olga are, at different times, treated as though they had no place in their own home. The only one she cannot really reach is Masha, who doesn't live in the house and who can in any case give as good as she gets. As part of her technique, Natasha's knack of not listening when it suits her is very highly developed. She has the most subtle way of putting down Andrei's pretensions to the intellectual life – she seems to regard his reading as being akin to playing with his toys – while her professed affection for Irina and Olga is hard to take seriously. Once married, she puts on airs, speaks bad French, and assumes that everyone would like to hear the latest news of her babies. Thereafter she seems to pop in from time to time only to remind us of petite-bourgeoise vulgarity. Having witnessed her abandonment of her children for the sake of a ride with Protopopov moments after she has cancelled the carnival, and then her foul treatment of Anfisa, we probably find her in the end impossible to endure.

When all is said and done, she does lack the depth of characterisation that Chekhov bestows on the Prozorovs – especially when towards the climax she keeps appearing at her window more like Punch than Judy. In fact, she is never onstage for very long: perhaps Chekhov is less interested in her for her own sake than for the catastrophic effect on Andrei of choosing any wrong woman. She certainly has no conceivable place in the final tableau, as Kulygin does, and by then she seems to belong almost to another style of writing – to Chekhov's earlier one-act plays or stories, in fact. Whereas one is usually extremely curious about the unseen life of his characters – what they would do in other situations than those of the play – it is difficult to have the same interest in Natasha, except perhaps about her unsavoury encounters with Protopopov. It is also difficult to imagine her in a situation in which one might feel sorry for her, outside of severe physical pain – and perhaps not even then.

This makes the actress's job exceptionally difficult, since she has to have that curiosity. Meanwhile the audience needs to believe that Natasha exists, and even experience moments when we see her as the devil with, if not the best tunes, at least some plausible ones – even if we wouldn't want to spend an evening with her. You couldn't say she was an inattentive mother. On carnival night she does have a sick child, and there is a deal of drunken singing going on. She is obviously sexually attractive to some degree. Her gauche remarks are perhaps just her way making things work socially; and it could be argued that her revenge on the snobbishly exclusive Prozorovs is overdue. Watching, you could make this case, but your heart probably wouldn't be in it.

THE PROZOROVS

OLGA

(AWLga SergAYevnah PROHZohroff)

Olga seems to have all the burdens of the oldest child with few of the benefits, not even the approval of her parents. If Andrei is in fact older than her and technically head of the family, he so conspicuously falls short that the job of holding them all together seems to fall to Olga – as does that of establishing the play's dominant theme, their longing to 'go home'.

She complains continuously of tiredness yet we don't tire of her, since we know that she is telling no more than the truth; and we are also intrigued. There is something of her inner life which is withheld, compared to that of her two younger sisters. We know that she has reached a point when almost any kind man would do as her husband, just for the sake of company: it's a philosophy she passes on to Irina when she advises her to marry Baron Tuzenbakh. But we don't know whether anything deeper in Olga has ever been touched. She is the deputy headmistress and seems to be a good teacher, as far as anyone can tell; less of a show-off than Kulygin, hardworking and thorough, she even gives lessons in the evenings. It seems no wonder her head aches all the time, and that she occasionally loses her temper with her pupils. Her diligence and public-spiritedness are evident on the night of the fire, when she is clearly at her best, apart from her failure to protect Anfisa – and to be fair, the strain of showing continual kindness to everyone else may be what makes her so feeble at that moment. Certainly she is more voluble and energetic here than anywhere else in the play, except at its ending.

Perhaps her worst moment, on the other hand, is her assault on Natasha's dress sense – one of those unthinking remarks that just slips out of her mouth before she can stop herself. I have seen it played that way and, since thoughtless cruelty hurts far more than calculated insult, it was much more painful for Natasha than if Olga had stopped in her tracks, expressed horror, and delivered the line in a considered way. The colour of a dress is a small thing in itself; but siblings sometimes have an instinctive prejudice against whoever is in love with one of them; simply the sight of Natasha has put Olga into such a defensive mode that she is hardly aware of herself.

She also, on occasion, seems a bit emotionally squeamish: you might say this is to do with her social conditioning, but it is noticeable that she tends to close her ears or remove herself at certain crucial moments. She dreads what Chebutykin is about to do when he goes off to get Irina's present in Act One:

Yes, it's awful. He's always doing something silly.

– and when the old man arrives with his samovar she even covers her face and leaves the room:

A samovar! This is terrible!

Perhaps the mundane present has stirred a deep upset in her at the limited hopes they all have.

With Masha it is worse still: Olga appears to be a strength for the middle sister, and then fails to be. When, much to everyone else's dismay, Masha threatens to go home on Irina's name-day, Olga just says:

I understand you, Masha . . .

However, when Masha wants to confide her feelings for Vershinin in Act Three, Olga's reaction is opposite: she goes behind the screen, says she won't listen, and even covers her ears.

Not that you can blame her when Masha finally holds onto Vershinin for dear life – 'Stop it, stop . . . ' – it is too painful to witness, and there are many people, including Mashas' husband, around. Accommodating Vershinin as he waited a moment before this was an admirable effort, however. It was also a preparation for the end, which echoes the opening of the play. Olga set the tone then, insisting that they can talk calmly about their father's death, and that it is even possible to wake up with happiness in your heart again. And what, after all, is the difference between this, in Act One:

> Oh, dear God, I woke up this morning, saw the light streaming in, the spring sunshine, and felt such joy welling up in my heart . . .

– and this, at the very end of Act Four:

> The band's playing so cheerfully, and I want to live so much! . . . Oh, dear heaven . . . No, my dear sisters, our lives aren't over yet. We must live!

The difference in one sense is a lifetime, but in another very little – the same voice and the same song, now drawing an unquenchable hope from tragic circumstances.

MASHA

(MARsha SerGAYevnah KoolEEGhina)

As we have seen, Chekhov offered more tips to Olga Knipper, playing Masha in the original production, than to anyone else, even though he also said 'I trust you, you're a good actress', as if they weren't necessary. His comments are extremely interesting, hinting at central things in the interpretation of all his characters. He insisted that Masha should look young and lively, be fond of laughing, though with a temper that is inclined to flare up. He writes from Nice during rehearsals:

> . . . do watch out. Don't look sad in any of the acts. You can look angry, that's all right, but not sad. People who have been unhappy for a long time, and grown used to it, don't get beyond whistling and are often wrapped up in their thoughts.

In other words, always look behind the obvious, and take what a person presents to the world not at face value but possibly as a defence, or at least the result of experience. Chekhov writes about what people have become, not what they always unalterably were.

So – Masha seems at first glance to be the most independent of the three sisters: she dresses eccentrically in black; whistles and hums in what is thought an unladylike way; interrupts conversation with murmured snatches of poetry; reads rather than talks to her sister on her name-day; and even threatens to leave before lunch on such an occasion. In fact, though, she is the most dependent on circumstance: while her sisters can get away to their jobs, she is stuck, grafted to Kulygin. Masha's nostalgia is not so much for Moscow as for the old days in general, when she was unmarried, their father was alive and their house (the present one as much as their Moscow home) was full of officers. When she does speak about those times she sounds the most snobbish: she complains about having to live nowadays in this place and climate, among such dreadful people. But her reminiscences are more vivid than those of her sisters: you can imagine her arriving home from the opera, dropping her shawl on the floor and calling for the servants. And she is talented – an accomplished pianist, though as Irina significantly remarks she hasn't played for 'three years . . . maybe four' (Is this a clue to Masha's age? Did she stop when she married Kulygin at eighteen or soon after? So is she about twenty-two in Act Three, when this is discussed?)

Her escape from the unwelcome present is of course more reckless than her sisters' – Vershinin. Having complained about having to listen to 'all this talk' (presumably from her husband's colleagues) it is the play's dubious speechifier that she falls for – but at least he does have a bit of style. She is so preoccupied with him that she is no help in the fire. For someone who complains about rudeness she is remarkably rude: 'Stop howling,' she snaps when Olga weeps; she openly attacks both Protopopov and Natasha (which is rather a relief); and she tells Vershinin on meeting that he has aged, though no doubt this is a defensive reaction to the fact that she is attracted to him.

Far more than her sisters, she tells the truth. This is not only apparent when she declares to Chebutykin that, for all her pretensions and sense of superiority, she feels the same as Martha their cook did about *her* man. She is the one who raises the problem of Andrei's debts when everyone else ignores it, and her confession of love, though ill-judged for the occasion, is both moving and wise.

And certainly we suffer with her, for all her acquired faults. For one thing, we can see that these are mistakes: she thinks knowing languages is unnecessary in such a town, but that is only because she is so worn down by the place, not because she seriously believes that to be a linguist is in itself bad. Listening to her obsession with the military, as opposed to the civilians, she doesn't like, we know she is misled: the dangerous and uncouth Soliony is one of her favoured group, and Vershinin, for all his charms, is probably less kind a man than her despised Kulygin. We feel for her when she tries to disobey Kulygin about visiting the headmaster but fails – who hasn't made a minor stand in life and then humiliatingly had to abandon it?

Her love affair is most delicately handled; we feel the warmth of it like a flickering fire in the cold room of her life. Her re-action to his first declaration is extremely human: she changes the subject, then moves him to where there is more light for him to see her eyes by, then asks him to stop, then to go on, then says it doesn't matter. We understand well why during so much of Act Two she laughs quietly to herself. Her presence quickens Vershinin to eloquence whenever they are together, and their hidden language – 'Tram-tam-tam' – as they wait to be united is sexy and charming. Her sense that love is an un-knowable experience until you encounter it is absolutely right:

> It's frightening, isn't it? Is it wrong? . . . What's to become of us? . . . when you fall in love yourself, it's obvious that nobody knows anything . . .

She is warning her inexperienced sister that to 'read a love story' in no way prepares you for an awesome experience which isolates you from the rest of the world rather than putting you in step with it.

Perhaps best of all, at the extreme moment when she struggles to hold on to her Pushkin quotes and Kulygin puts on his false moustache, she manages:

> Actually, you do look like the German teacher.

You admire the superhuman effort, at the same time as you might think her wilful and self-centred for having carried on her affair under his nose.

In the end she is a Prozorov – 'we must live, we must' – and criticism fades away because of the author's affection for her, and the overwhelmingly human quality of what she experiences.

IRINA

(EerEEna SergAYevna PrOHzohroff, 'IREEnooshka')

A golden girl in white, twenty years old, announces in her first line that it is bad to dwell on the past – 'Why bring it all back?' – and then spends much of the play trying to do just that. Irina's sense of the contrast between past and present is one of her most powerful emotions. But whereas Andrei, for instance, seems content to dwell on the past for its own sake, she wants to bring it all back to propel her into the future – into a return to Moscow and a renewed life. Her fragile plans are sincerely encouraged by the assiduous Tuzenbakh, who may or may not be thinking of Moscow as the base for their idealised new life together.

When a young person insists they are grown up it is the most youthful thing about them. So Irina denies how young she is, but immediately squeals with delight when Fedotik gives her crayons and a penknife. She also sounds her age when she describes her feelings to Chebutykin:

It's as if I'm sailing, with a wide deep sky above me and great white birds flying past

and, in the same tone, eulogises the life of labour:

it must be wonderful to be a workman . . . or a shepherd, or a teacher, teaching children, or an engine-driver on the railway.

She looks especially young next to Vershinin, both before he arrives –

Is he old? . . . Is he an interesting person?

– and in his company. He is so much more worldly, so much older in experience, and her response to his speechifying is quite schoolgirlish:

We really ought to have noted all that down.

The first impression then is of a delightful girl, on the threshold of her life, but one who as yet knows herself the least.

However her little scene with Tuzenbakh, as they go into lunch at the end of Act One, extends our understanding of the tension within her. Here she strikes the first negative notes of her part: she doesn't want Tuzenbakh to talk to her of love, and firmly denies the beauty of life – far from being beautiful to her and her sisters, it has 'trampled us down, like weeds'. This ugly thought brings her to the edge of tears – which she resists, and then immediately swings into her hopes of a future full of useful work. Her optimism is in direct proportion to her sorrow.

In the second act it is quite shocking to see the latter quality taking over. She arrives home exhausted from a job that has no poetry, and gives Tuzenbakh less than no encouragement, her head full of the episode with the bereaved woman and of Andrei's profligacy. It is as if five years, not one or two, have passed: her voice is, so to speak, deeper, more considered, older. Only Chebutykin, the father-figure – and perhaps indeed her father – can cheer her up and make her young again. She doesn't criticise Natasha, though she suffers most from her restless reorganising of the bedrooms. She is seriously frightened by Soliony, whom her instincts read quite correctly while the others think him a buffoon, and her brooding mood holds together the comings and goings in the act's last few minutes. But she is the same girl: as the last line shows, her longing to return to Moscow is as strong as ever.

She goes from the telegraph office to the town council. It is the thought of Andrei, the other bureaucrat, that sparks her harrowing breakdown in Act Three – an unanswerable catalogue of failure about which she can no longer deceive herself. Then we see her, in Act Four, on the day before her wedding. She still says little that is critical about Natasha – even as she is preparing to leave, she describes the agony of living in the house now that Olga has left as no more than being:

> on my own, bored stiff, with nothing to do, and that hateful room I have to live in.

And we surely admire her courage in stating the terms of their marriage so clearly to Tuzenbakh – she can't love him, she will be faithful and supportive, but her heart is locked up like a piano without a key. If it wasn't that we know where Tuzenbakh is headed, it would be a most moving display of how far she has come since she was twenty.

Irina's journey through the play illustrates perfectly the difficulty of making final judgments about Chekhov's characters: she seems a simple enough proposition, but really she is an odd combination of youth and maturity. She is very naive but also makes fun of herself for liking to stay in bed until twelve, drinking coffee and then spending two hours dressing (a part-exaggeration which Olga immediately corrects). As the youngest sister, she lived for a shorter time in Moscow than her siblings, but her nostalgia for it is the sharpest: she is the one who supplies the detail of where they lived, on Old Basmanny Street, and she makes a point of telling Vershinin that their mother is buried in Moscow. In fact it is Irina who thinks most often of her dead mother, having the freshest memories of her face from when she was a baby. Above all, she has the self-knowledge of the true heroine, and she is hardest on herself – a necessary balance to her youthful optimism.

To watch the light of hope going out in a girl of Irina's age is a particularly painful thing, in life as in the play. The youngest child, protected and full of possibilities, of whom, as of Andrei, so much might be expected, becomes as weakened by events as he does. But at two crucial moments, Chekhov gives her exactly the same stage direction. Both when in Act Three Olga advises her to marry the Baron, and again when she is brought the news of his death at the end, Irina 'quietly weeps'. So the youngest sister is asked to make the least fuss in her laments, silently crying like someone older, rather than howling like a child. There is no excess, just deep and – for the moment – inconsolable distress. My guess is that Chekhov wants us to see her as on the brink of real maturity, and, surprisingly enough, the one most able to face the future – when she will give her life to those who need it, in the belief that even without Tuzenbakh she can live a life she can be proud of. As she says at the very start: 'God willing, it'll all work out'. I think it will.

ANDREI

(AhndRAY SergAYevitch PROHZohroff – AndrYOOsha)

It is not clear how old Andrei is, or where he stands in the order of Prozorov births. He has been to Moscow University, of which he has vivid memories in Act Two, having even been looking at his lectures from those days. His sisters think he has it in him to go back as a Professor – an enormous idea in the Russia of that time, comparable to being a military general: nowadays it is a little more commonplace. Olga says 'they' left Moscow eleven years ago, but whether that included him, or whether he stayed behind to study, or returned to the city later, is not clear. He is certainly expected to take the lead in the family, acting as his dead father's heir, but this may simply be because he is the only male.

There is however something about him – or his sisters' attitude to him – that makes it intriguing to imagine him as other than the eldest. Their glorification could very easily be of the spoiling kind for the cherished younger brother. Unfortunately this cosseting also makes Andrei a victim: they are turning him into something he really isn't. Actor and director will need to decide his age and real capacities, as well as just how good a violinist he is.

There does appear to be a lack of will in Andrei; our first encounter with him strikes a dispiriting note after all the build up. It's not just that he is a little overweight, perspiring and short of sleep – that is normal enough. But we gradually sense how biased his sisters are. He is slightly dismissive to Vershinin about their enthusiasm for anybody who comes from Moscow, and having done the bare minimum conversationally he escapes as soon as he can – it is a little impolite. He is then not there to greet Natasha when she arrives, though she certainly needs him to break the ice for her. His attraction to her, so passionately expressed, is surprising – although pretty clearly, their match is for him a means of escape, an ill-judged attempt to take charge of his own life. Just as he lacked the strength to resist his sisters' teasing, he will not feel able to stand up to his increasingly controlling wife, whether over the children, the carnival party, or the money he has borrowed from the bank. He would rather escape, first into his study to his violin, and later, far more damagingly, to the gambling tables.

He feels, in his own words, 'alone, and alien'; in a way he is most naturally himself when he talks to the deaf Ferapont, the equivalent of thinking aloud in an empty room. He slips into the Act Two gathering quietly, still reading, but then has his one moment of release, when the infectious high spirits of Tuzenbakh make him dance and sing a silly song. It doesn't last: Natasha puts a stop to it, and he can't manage to arbitrate between her and the revellers. Furtively, complaining about marriage and short-windedness, he slips away with Chebutykin to whatever gambling-house this town offers.

The sisters are soon complaining that he has become old and mean-spirited – they are angry in proportion to their earlier enthusiasm. They are especially aggrieved that he hasn't helped with the fire and has allowed Natasha to pocket the mortgage money – not that they are any better at dealing with her than he is. When he arrives to say his piece, he is trying to re-make the world as he wants it to be – a nostalgic world in which Natasha is a fine, honest woman, upright and honourable, loved by them as well as by him.

But by this time, having been the daily beauty in their lives, he has become someone they can hardly bear to look at. It is pitiful, although his character does turn a corner when he breaks down and admits his hypocrisy: 'Don't believe a word of it'. For the rest of the play, despite his humiliations, he achieves a little shambolic dignity, haunting Act Four like a ghost, and taking a small stand about the immorality of Chebutykin's involvement in the duel. He confides in Chebutykin that his wife is like 'a blind furry animal . . . not human', which is honest, as is his admission that he still loves her without knowing why. Elsewhere, he is oddly loyal to Natasha: he says nothing negative about her to anyone else. When he finally finds his voice, late in the play, he laments his own failures, to be sure, but earns our respect by quickly moving on to a powerfully coherent – and, we guess, accurate – verdict on the society in which he finds himself. He ends it as he did in Act Three, with sheer helpless love for his sisters, and effectively disappears from the play, though the image of him endlessly pushing his pram continues to haunt it. Significantly, he is not included in the final central tableau but stays on the periphery – we have virtually forgotten him as the sisters come together. Perhaps his character is too complex and unresolved to lend much to this climactic moment: after all, he has always absented himself when an emotional climax was brewing.

In summary, little of what Andrei does could be called a crime – he is merely a disappointment, and to nobody more than himself. He may, as Chebutykin advises, pack his bag and walk away; or more likely he will stay, struggling on, with a little more dignity for having unburdened himself of his feelings. As his children grow up perhaps he will retire and even take up the violin again. He is shy, talented, self-effacing, and he makes a bad marriage. It is a common enough story.

THE ARMY

LIEUTENANT COLONEL VERSHININ

(AlexSARNder IgNAHtyehvitch VershEEnin)

Battery Commander Vershinin is a mystery. He enters the play much heralded, almost as if he were to be the central character, and immediately impresses with his mixture of social polish and polite curiosity. It has an intriguing, slightly melancholy undertone:

> My, how you've grown! ... Yes, time flies all right! ...
> I need only close my eyes and I can see him, [their father]
> as large as life.

This impression of sensitivity deepens as he tells the story of his days as the 'love-sick major', staring down into the river from the 'gloomy-looking bridge' on the way to his Moscow barracks. It is an easy step from that to ruminations on time sweeping everything away on its remorseless current. His appreciation of nature – the 'gentle, modest' birch trees and the house full of flowers – and his insistence that intellectual accomplishment, taken for granted by Andrei and Masha, is worth something, make him seem particularly soulful. No wonder Masha takes off her hat and stays to lunch; no wonder he has no difficulty in getting himself invited to supper as well; and no wonder Masha decides that the most 'decent, the most honourable and well-bred people' in the town are soldiers such as he. It is a piece of luck for him to find such a willing audience: he must be quite taken aback by the sisters' wild enthusiasm for his memories of Moscow and of their family. It makes his path into their hearts relatively easy. How many times has he been posted in a provincial town, needing to make an impression on the local gentry; this time, however, he has found people who have a real connection with him.

And that is where the trouble starts. It is inevitable that someone should fall for Vershinin: Irina might seem the most likely to, but she is rather young for him, whereas Masha has at least some experience of life. Even she is no match for his accomplished wooing. And is he a little too accomplished? There is nothing wrong with his philosophising, but it can be imprecise: his gift of the gab is attractive, but there is a sneaking feeling that it is calculated to arouse sympathy and prepare for seduction. He seems to turn it on like a tap, then off again when it has done the trick. Accustomed to creating a succession of intrigues to distract him from his life at home, is he now taking ample advantage of Masha?

To answer this, we start to comb his scenes for clues. Why is his wife so angry with him? Why is he so extremely negative about her – not a word of understanding – whilst having a sentimental attitude to his children, whom he seems to neglect. How does Tuzenbakh know from the start that he will talk about her, unless this is his habitual tactic, as in 'My wife doesn't understand me'? Why does he start a debate with Tuzenbakh and then leave him conversationally stranded? Is his tact in refusing to join in Masha's denunciation of her husband and his colleagues in Act Two simply a device to lead her on? He goes on to puncture her affectations: as far as he is concerned, there is nothing so special about the military that she admires so much. As for her nostalgia for Moscow, there is his story of the government minister in his prison cell. Is this tough love, or callous indifference to her feelings? And finally, is his departure a well-worn routine or does he feel real distress?

In the end the audience may conclude the case is not proved, or argue about it later. Chekhov has done his usual balancing act by not passing judgment and making us hesitate to as well. Put simply, Vershinin never owns up. In this play, most of the major characters have their moment of confession – most obviously the Prozorovs and Chebutykin. Kulygin exposes his innermost feelings indirectly but unmistakably. Tuzenbakh is in a constant state of confession to Irina. The exceptions are Natasha, who hardly needs to do such a thing, her objectives being so evident; Soliony, who is presented two-dimensionally though suggestively; and Vershinin, from whom you might expect it. The actor playing him may (as I did) find this a little frustrating. The part is a pleasure to do, as most Chekhovs are, but you know you are presenting an enigma whose main purpose in the play is to have an effect. Much as the actor will want to establish a point of view, the decision will always be arbitrary. If there were to be an improvisation exercise in rehearsals in which Vershinin is cross-examined on his motives as if on trial, he might have to take the Fifth Amendment when asked about his previous offences. He might rest his case on the difficulties of the military life: whatever he has done is what life has forced on him, and in any case, he might claim, he really did go on writing to Masha from Poland, whether or not the letters arrived.

LIEUTENANT THE BARON TUZENBAKH

(NikolEYE Lvovvich Toozenbakh)
This would be the stress in German; in Russian, as he would no doubt prefer, it would be more like ToozenBAKH

Even the cynical Chebutykin says he is 'a fine chap'. The affectionate Irina describes him as 'a fine man . . . an extraordinarily fine man'; Olga says he is decent and clean-living.

He plays the piano with feeling, and therefore has the authority to say that Masha has talent on the same instrument, and
he will not hear of anyone doubting it. He is humorous about
Vershinin's foibles and patient with Soliony – he even has
some sympathy for him, until (out of our sight) his patience
snaps and he provokes the fatal duel. He is humorous too
about his German name, which seems to set him apart, despite
his longing to be a part of this group and of Russia's future.
His wish to escape his privileged background for a poorer and
more honest life is attractive if a little romantic; indeed it may
be thanks to that background that he is so sociable and good-
natured. Courteous too: he is the only regular at lunch in Act
One who does not tease Natasha or Andrei. His love of Irina,
for whom he would give his life (and in fact does), and his
appetite for the idea of work, are agreeably merged: he is
barely able to mention one without the other. There seems to
be complete agreement about how nice he is.

But fate is unkind, and there is an equal consensus about
Tuzenbakh's plainness and lack of charisma. The women are
used to him in his uniform but they find him comic in his civilian suit, even though in a stage direction Chekhov insists that
it is 'fashionable'. Intelligent though his conversation may be,
it hasn't Vershinin's energy or style. Next to him, Tuzenbakh
just lacks a certain magnetism.

He is of course a great talker nonetheless, and one of the two
central strands in his story is his frequent speculation with
Vershinin about the future of Russia. Tuzenbakh makes two
attempts to define his position in Act One. First he believes
that the present generation can hold its head up and will be
remembered with respect for progress made – no torture or
executions (not quite true), and a 'rise in moral standards',
despite the surrounding sufferings. Then he insists that life
will eventually become more 'beautiful and astonishing', but
only if everyone works hard now to prepare the way, creating
a stake for themselves in that future. He returns to the fray in
Act Two. Humorously, he suggests all sorts of new-fangled
inventions ahead – spiritualism, aerial balloons – but declares
that people will still be complaining that life's mixture is
'difficult, full of mystery, and happy'. He insists that this

happiness even exists now, largely because nothing can be known: life continues obliviously, we no more understand our actions than do the cranes who keep flying, and we would be foolish to enquire into the meaning of a snowfall. This is the happiness of passivity, or like Socrates saying he is wise bcause he knows nothing, and a little surprising given Tuzenbakh's appetite for intellectual enquiry. Even Masha finds such a philosophy – a life without evident meaning – intolerable.

More pungently, he predicts with uncanny accuracy the 'fierce cleansing wind' that is 'blowing up' in Russia: he says that in twenty-five or thirty years everyone will work. In 1917 the Russian Revolution would be that wind; at the end of 1922 the Soviet Union would be founded, dedicated to such an idea of labour. Perhaps because of this accuracy, it is sometimes thought that Tuzenbakh may be expressing Chekhov's own hopes; but this is far too subtle a writer for that, and if he has an opinion it is spread on both sides of the argument.

The other strand in Tuzenbakh is of course his absolute devotion to Irina, dogged and even a little dog-like. His persistence has something heroic about it, though in every other way he lacks the traditional qualities of a hero. Such complete self-surrender, punctuated by the most lyrical descriptions of her 'wonderful, fascinating hair' and her 'beautiful eyes', her face that 'lights up the night air, like a moonbeam' and the 'long, long line of days' ahead for their love, may be wearisome to her when she is in the wrong mood. But they are her salvation next to the compliments of Soliony, which are violent and without tenderness. Tuzenbakh's love is presented throughout very touchingly (and sometimes comically), down to the final moments when he refuses to tell her where he is going and wants her to reward him with some word of love. He goes to his death with a marvellous apprehension of the natural life around him and a mystical instinct for where he will fit into it: in these moments of generosity, self-denial and spiritual alertness, he seems, without looks or prospects, preferable to almost everyone in the play.

MILITARY DOCTOR CHEBUTYKIN

(EevAHn RomAHnitch ChebootEEkin)

The initial impression of Chebutykin is of an eccentric and lovable uncle. He enters the play with a handful of anecdotes – home cures for falling hair, and a nameless use for a bottle, a glass tube and some alum – and is soon demonstrating his extreme fondness for and indulgence of Irina. There would seem to be some laziness in him, but he is nearly sixty after all, old at that time, and it is rendered charming by his frank admission of it: he says he hasn't opened a book since he left university, so even his newspaper-reading is limited to non-literary subjects. All the same, there's something vainglorous about his profession of ignorance, as if it was a front he's decided to adopt. His present of the samovar to his beloved is seen by Olga as a 'terrible' thing (she even has to leave the room in embarrassment), by Masha as shameless, and by Irina as far too expensive. It is inappropriate, certainly, but his emotional outburst when it misfires is likely to endear him to the audience, since it was all based on his love for Irina and her dead mother.

The first real hint that all is not quite well with him comes in the guise of a joke: Tuzenbakh may think that future gener-ations will look up to the present, but Chebutykin feels he is physically too small for that compliment, and he senses that Tuzenbakh is only saying that life has meaning in order to cheer him up. Then he returns to his benevolent role. At the end of the first act he teases Andrei and Natasha with quotes from comic opera, but no more, and no more cruelly, than everyone else; and the second act sustains the impression of a highly-indulged, permanent member of the household. Though he is billeted here, unlike the other soldiers, he is easily forgiven for not paying his rent and Irina spoils him with constant games of patience. He quotes from his paper, pre-tends he is thirty-two, seems not particularly upset by his disagreement with Soliony about *chehartma*, and sings and dances with the rest. Natasha may choose him as the one to whom to whisper the news that the carnival party isn't coming because he is the least likely to resist her. But as the revelry breaks up, something more distinct about him emerges. As he prepares to go gambling with Andrei, he admits how much he loved the Prozorovs' mother, though she was married, and so he himself 'never got round to marrying'. Unlike Andrei, who has, Chebutykin thinks it must be a better state than the loneliness he feels. Then he utters for the first time what will become, in various re-phrasings, a terrible refrain:

well, does it really matter?

Ominously, he seems incapable of giving Andrei even the simplest medical advice for his breathlessness. This failure of professional memory partly cues his next appearance, drunk on the night of the fire. But whereas having forgotten everything seemed to be a joke with Andrei, the death of a patient has now made it a torment. The self-laceration and disgust of this outburst, so inappropriate in its timing and so full of hatred for the world around him, is very shocking. Still, if the production has delicately established his lack of self-worth, his sense of intellectual failure and his disappointed love, an audience will realise how his demons have come to control him after a drink: the same demons insist that salvation lies in a brutal frankness about Natasha's affair with Protopopov.

The scar of Act Three is evident in Act Four: both his resignation and his chilling way of covering it up are featured. He complains gently of having been forgotten, looks forward to retirement and a reformed way of life, once again expresses his love for Irina, and is a confidant for Masha, without quite admitting the relationship he may have had with her mother. But when the big crises come, he relapses into a sort of offensive indifference. What does it matter what happened on the boulevard yesterday? It's 'all bunkum . . . ta-ra-ra boom-de-ay'; it 'hardly matters' whether he comes back next year or not; who cares whether Tuzenbakh lives or dies, we're not here anyway, it's just an illusion.

By now we understand the roots of this cynicism, and have reinterpreted what once seemed lovable: most jolly people are covering something. Chebutykin's newspaper-reading and note-taking were his way of not engaging with what he didn't like. And still at the centre of his life is his hopeless love for Irina's mother, with its unresolved hint that he might be Irina's father.

The actor must have confidence that we understand all this, and play the final brutal moments for all they are worth. We will see them for what they are, and the musical pattern of the play certainly requires a hard counterpoint to the emotion expressed by the sisters. On the other hand, if the actor keeps reminding us of the distress beneath Chebutykin's callousness, there will be too much sentiment on the stage. Audiences are intelligent: they can draw their own conclusions. Chekhov had faith in this, and he knew that it is often best to express an emotion by means of an action, even if it is only the folding or unfolding of a newspaper, and even if it seems to be the opposite of the truth.

SECOND CAPTAIN SOLIONY

(Vasilyee VaseELyevitch SolyAWny).

If Chekhov were to deal in theatrical stereotypes, Captain Soliony, the cause of the play's final catastrophe, would be, with Natasha, the villain of the piece. He is certainly an odd man out, and socially embarrassing. His ominous silences, desire to disconcert, inappropriate quotations and non sequiturs make him unsettling company, often funny but in a slightly alarming way. But it is interesting for the audience – and essential for the actor – to notice the rare moments when Chekhov's generosity stretches even to him, inviting us to consider his complicated personality:

> When I'm alone with someone, it's fine . . . but in company I get depressed and withdrawn . . . I say all kinds of stupid things.

This, after all, is the standard complaint of the shy person, one who hates parties or noisy gatherings. It shows a self-consciousness which is itself a form of pride, and may indeed come across as arrogance. The actor looking for Soliony's positive qualities will notice that, much as he poses as the misunderstood outsider, he has his moments of self-knowledge. But they are usually tainted with some less-attractive, competitive quality. Even as he confides in Tuzenbakh about his feelings of alienation, he insists that it is not enough for him to be as good as the people around him. He must be even better:

> Still, I'm as decent and honourable as the next man, a great deal more so, indeed. And I can prove it.

He doesn't quite do that, but he does occasionally have the gift of candour. Both the audience and his onstage colleagues may have a sneaking regard for someone who deals with Natasha's conceited prattling about Bobik not with false politeness but with the desire to fry him up in a pan and eat him. He is also quite well-read: where Vershinin, the senior officer, feels he doesn't know how to choose books and so reads the wrong ones, Soliony knows his Lermontov and his Pushkin – and writes his own poetry, though we don't know what it's like.

He is, in fact, a mass of nineteenth-century Russian complexes quite hard for us to grasp. In his correspondence, Chekhov rather enigmatically points out:

> Soliony really does think he looks like Lermontov, but of course he doesn't, it's absurd to think of such a thing . . . he must be made up to look like Lermontov. He has a great resemblance to Lermontov, but this resemblance exists only in Soliony's mind.

He seems to be saying here that though in one way it is ridiculous for Soliony to think of himself like that, he is as entitled as anyone else to his private fantasies. On the other hand, Soliony's tendency to tease (to put it mildly), and to manufacture small conflicts where none really exist, is obviously likely to lead to serious trouble in the end. He even comes into the play with his horns mildly locked with Tuzenbakh – we don't know what he has said, but it is enough to make the mild-mannered Baron declare it such 'nonsense' that he is 'fed up listening' to him.

As well as having it in for Tuzenbakh, Soliony has a tense relationship with Chebutykin. He starts by exchanging anecdotes with the older man: his account of the odd 'fact' that two men are more than twice as strong as one is really a way of boasting of his own physical strength. Then he has another go at Chebutykin by apparently declaring that he will blow his brains out one day – something he ends up doing to the unfortunate Tuzenbakh. In the second act, which he enters alone, he has two silly arguments with the doctor, about Caucasian food and the number of universities in Moscow.

He doesn't appear to mind saying foolish things in front of his superior officer Vershinin, to whom he makes the poor joke about the railway station and even insists that the Prozorovs' liqueur is made from cockroaches. So he is in some way the licensed fool in the group. Much of the time he is asserting himself to impress Irina. At the end of Act Two, the reason for his constant niggling at the Baron becomes obvious: he emerges as an extremely alarming suitor for her. His wooing is claustrophobic and threatening, most unlike Tuzenbakh's:

> You're the only one who understands me . . . I can't live without you . . .

There is something fanatical about this, deeply uncomfortable for the woman even if she were not already involved; and his threat to kill any rival is a simple prophecy.

Soliony makes only one appearance in Act Three, when he is asked to leave the room because of his overpowering cologne and his general awkwardness. He interprets this as favouritism towards Tuzenbakh, and it is enough to tighten the tension in Act Four. It seems that the Baron has lost his temper at last and insulted Soliony. Perhaps Soliony wanted this – an excuse to kill his rival with a semblance of justice. It would be part of his antiquated code of honour that such a thing must lead to a duel, so he would say he was only doing the right thing. On his way to the showdown he is forcedly cheerful with Chebutykin, promises only to 'wing' the Baron, but is nervous enough to have used up a whole bottle of scent on his hands, which 'smell like a corpse'. It is a human as well as symbolic touch; he then goes on his deadly way, making a sidelong reference to Lermontov's poem *The Sail*, a celebration of the Romantic Outsider par excellence:

> 'Forget, forget thy dreams'.

Quite possibly, he meant to keep his promise, to wound and not to kill. He will certainly have no chance of continuing his courtship of Irina, as they are headed in different directions. For someone who lives in a fantasy world, it is hard to know if Soliony has really worked out such practicalities. It may be that at the critical moment he couldn't resist the melodrama of it, a chance at last to become a real anti-hero with bloodied hands. Perhaps, he thinks, someone will write a poem about him one day.

Altogether, Soliony is a retrograde character, a dark shadow running through the play. His hero is a Byronic poet, dead for half a century, and his dream of duels is more appropriate to the early nineteenth century than the beginning of the twentieth (Lermontov himself died in a duel in 1841). Chekhov keeps the writing of the part quite brief – it is relatively small, as if we were not meant to delve too deeply into Soliony's character or motivations. We are encouraged to see him primarily as a narrative element, kept human enough by his idiosyncrasies and his share in the prevailing disease of the group – a tendency to fall victim to their own idea of themselves.

FEDOTIK

(Alexei Pehtrawvitch Fehdawtik, Sub-Lieutenant)

The younger officers, Fedotik and Rodé, form background music to the scenes they are in, and it should be played as warmly and sympathetically as possible. Although they are junior, they seem to be on easy and relaxed terms with Vershinin and their other superiors. In fact it is a feature of the play that the atmosphere seems so non-hierarchical that Soliony can make silly jokes and interrupt Vershinin without anybody minding very much.

Second Lieutenant Fedotik seems a delightful man, a compulsive giver of presents, especially to Irina, with whom he might be a little in love. But it is a harmless love, and he is equally kind to Kulygin at the beginning of Act Four, presenting him with much the same gifts – a notebook and pencil – that he habitually gives to her. Within moments of arriving in the play, he is presenting flowers, taking photographs (still quite a novelty at the time), and producing the greatest novelty of all, a spinning top that hypnotises everyone at lunch. In the second act, he and Rodé provide a very specific mood by singing to the guitar behind the philosophical discussion. Irina seems to sing along with them, and is rewarded with more gifts, coloured pencils and a penknife with several blades:

> One's for cleaning out your ears, and this one's for your fingernails . . .

– as well as a new kind of patience; and Fedotik is familiar enough with Irina to say that she won't go to Moscow because the cards aren't coming out.

He is above all open and unprejudiced. When the carnival party is cancelled, his flexibility is in quite sharp contrast to all the discontent around him. The problems of the family simply wash over him:

> . . . if the child's sick, well, of course . . . I'll bring him a toy tomorrow . . .

But his finest moment comes in the fire, when he laughs and dances because all his belongings are burned – his guitar, his camera, his letters, and, perhaps worst of all, a little notebook he was going to give Irina. He seems to have found another camera by the beginning of Act Four (as well as a notebook for Kulygin), and what he brings to this act is an unexpected toughness – he is insistent that this is the end, that the group of friends will never be together again. He is a realist, and self-confident enough to become irritated that the others won't hold still for their photograph. So his final moments make it impossible for us to think of him only as an eccentric or a joker.

RODE

(VladEEmir KARPovich RAWday, Sub-Lieutenant).

Perhaps to make up for the fact that Chekhov has given him less to say and fewer appearances, Rodé does have, apart from his French name, one big character trait: he shouts, in a guttural

accent. Who knows why, but he does. The point is insisted on
before each of his utterances in Act One: for some reason he
has been out walking with Kulygin's high school boys, 'teaching them gymnastics', so perhaps he hasn't yet adjusted his
volume. In Act Two both his remarks are to be uttered 'loudly'.

He is a little less sympathetic than Fedotik – he complains at
the cancellation of the party in the standard way, with no reference to the baby:

> I mean, it's only just nine o'clock.

He feels particularly aggrieved because he has had a special
rest in preparation for a wild night of dancing.

In Act Four he starts (and perhaps continues) the call of
'Cooo-eee' that becomes such a haunting refrain, leaving the
play with it; and he is at one with Fedotik about the finality of
things. He is obviously there as part of a duet: noticeably he
and Fedotik are 'noisily welcomed' by everyone at the lunch
table in Act One, so they are clearly much approved of. They
are the kind of friends, sociable and harmless, that many
families depend on. But overall it may be that Rodé's disconcerting loudness and relative lack of warmth is devised by
Chekhov to balance the obvious amiability of his colleague.

THE SERVANTS

FERAPONT

(FehrahPAWnt)

By the time of *Three Sisters*, Chekhov was becoming very alert
to the possibilities of a deaf character both for harmless
liberating comedy and a certain kind of meaning. In this sense
old Ferapont, 'watchman for the local council', is a forerunner
of the great character of Firs in *The Cherry Orchard*, who at
one moment will appear to hear nothing or the wrong thing,
and will then give an exactly accurate answer to a straight
question.

Like that of Firs, Ferapont's deafness is variable. In the first
act he hears neither the message he is to take to Protopopov

about the cake nor the good news that he will get a piece himself ('What's that? . . . What?'). But when Andrei uses him as an unreliable sounding board in Act Two, Ferapont some-times grasps exactly what is under discussion. He seems to catch little of Andrei's early remarks – he is either unable to hear exactly or imagines that something has been said when it hasn't – but the word 'Moscow' sharpens his senses wonder-fully. He suddenly remembers, with an old man's mixture of waywardness and precision, that he has heard that there is a rope stretched right across the city, and that someone once ate forty pancakes there and dropped dead. Or it might have been fifty. It is all a preparation for his finest moment, when he answers the question about whether he has ever been to Moscow with disconcerting directness – 'It's not been God's will'. This is a quality of realism lacking in the sisters, who continue to yearn hopelessly for Moscow in defiance of the probability that God's will applies to them as well.

One of Ferapont's tasks is to pepper the play with anecdotes – Napoleon's advance on Moscow in 1812, then two hundred degrees of frost killing off two thousand people in St Peters-burg – or was it Moscow? But his main job is to be Andrei's shadow, and this is where the meaning of his presence in the play becomes a little deeper. To insist on an answer to whether the firemen can go through the garden when his master is in high distress may be funny, but it is also a necessary dramatic counterpoint to Andrei's emotionalism. Life simply has to go on, even if deafness allows you to ignore some of it; it is all very well to philosophise and lament, but papers must be signed as surely as night follows day. In this way this immov-able figure introduces into the drama the steadier rhythms – commonplace, unavoidable and endlessly repeated – of every-day life.

ANFISA

(AnFEESa)

If Ferapont looks forward to Firs in *The Cherry Orchard*, the family's nanny Anfisa continues a brief line in imperturbable old female retainers started by Marina in *UncleVanya*. This time her age is specified, and it is quite something: she is eighty, younger than Firs (87), but still, whatever Natasha may say, capable of useful work. She could well have been a nanny to the sisters' parents as well.

Like Marina in the earlier play, Anfisa is inclined to complain that mealtimes are being disrupted by the comings and goings in the household. Not knowing about Mrs Vershinin's suicide attempt, she is particularly irritated that Vershinin (whose name she tends to forget) leaves without having his tea. But she is still playing mother hen to the youngest child, Irina, and she is not entirely impervious to what is going on in the family: she is well aware of Andrei's general malaise ('He just sits there') and wisely does no more than whisper to Irina the contentious news that the now-superfluous carnival party has arrived.

Unlike Marina though, and a little surprisingly, she is not used as a point of stillness round which the play's emotions can swirl, or even as a source of common sense. Her main dramatic purpose is to occasion the unpleasant moment when the new usurps the old and Natasha throws her out of Olga's bedroom when she is resting (in the middle of the night, and having done much more to help than Natasha herself). Natasha's complaint that Anfisa shouldn't be in the house at all is a moment of great value in understanding Olga as well. And Anfisa's unwitting revenge is the one pleasure of the final act: tucked away in her warm rent-free flat at the school, near to Olga and forever safe from Natasha, she thinks she has died and gone to heaven.

These older roles in Chekhov should not be overlooked. They should be as strongly cast as possible, and have real character. Whether providing a quiet comment on the restless emotions about them or bearing witness to the play's historical moment, they provide a necessary perspective, their age and peasant dignity suggesting the merciless continuation of things.